I0079321

Purpose

Finding and Fulfilling the Will of God
for Our Lives and Churches

Malcolm Webber

Published by:

Strategic Press
www.StrategicPress.org

Strategic Press is a division of Strategic Global Assistance, Inc.
www.sgai.org

513 S. Main St. Suite 2
Elkhart, IN 46516
U.S.A.

+1-844-532-3371 (LEADER-1)

Copyright © 2001 Malcolm Webber

ISBN 978-1-888810-63-9

All Scripture references are from the New International Version of the Bible, unless otherwise noted.

Printed in the United States of America

Contents

Introduction

Someone once said, "Efforts and courage are not enough without purpose and direction."

My oldest son, John, tried to teach me how to play a particular card game. He explained this rule and that rule: "Dad, you take this card…and then that card…this card is worth this…and that card is worth that." I kept saying to him, "Well, that's fine, but what's the object of the game?"

What is the objective of what you are doing?

You may know all the rules and all the strategies, but if you don't know what the objective of the game is, you'll never win. All that other stuff won't help you. But when you do know the objective, then all the rest is of use to you.

Many Christians are like that. They have a great understanding of many of the "rules" of Christianity, but they don't know what the object is. They don't know what their purpose is in living the Christian life.

Think of running a race. You may have the best running shoes money can buy, and know all about how to breathe, and how to run, and even be in great physical condition, but if you don't know where the finish line is, you're in trouble!

Perhaps you would just follow the crowd? This is what many people in church do. They just follow the crowd, with no great sense of purpose or direction.

Sometimes following the crowd will work, but many times it will not work. What if those in the crowd don't know where they're going either? Just because there's a crowd doesn't mean they're going in the right direction.

Someone has said, "Do not follow where the path may lead. Go instead where there is no path and leave a trail."

Early in life, an aunt took former President Ronald Reagan to a cobbler to have a pair of shoes made for him. The shoemaker asked young Ronald, "Do you want a square toe or a round toe?" Reagan hemmed and hawed. So the cobbler said, "Come back in a day or two and let me know what you want." A few days later, the shoemaker saw Reagan on the street and asked what he had decided about the shoes. "I still haven't made up my mind," the boy answered. "Very well," said the cobbler. When Reagan received the shoes, he was shocked to see that one shoe had a square toe and the other a round toe. Years later, Reagan said, "Looking at those shoes every day taught me a lesson. If you don't make your own decisions, somebody else will make them for you!"

We must know our direction – our purpose. When we know our purpose we can have focus, and when we have focus, we can achieve our goals and accomplish God's will for our lives and for our churches.

Malcolm Webber, Ph.D.
Strategic Press
2000

Chapter 1

The Need for Purpose

The word of the Lord came to me, saying, "Before I formed you in the womb I knew you, before you were born I set you apart; I appointed you as a prophet to the nations." (Jer. 1:4-5)

(God) has saved us and called us to a holy life – not because of anything we have done but because of his own purpose and grace. This grace was given us in Christ Jesus before the beginning of time, (2 Tim. 1:9)

Before the world began, God gave you grace. This means your salvation and eternal life. Furthermore, He also gave you purpose before the world began. God gave you a purpose: a purpose for living, a purpose for being saved, a purpose for serving Him.

He gave you a purpose: a reason for living, a goal to achieve; and He gave you the grace to fulfill it. Thus, the more clearly you understand your purpose, the more closely you will be connected with God's grace to fulfill it.

So, what is your purpose? Who are you? What are you called to do with your life?

Many people just float through life and never ask these questions. They bounce from event to event in their lives, hopping from one stage of life to the next stage of life: "I'm born, then I'm a child, I start going to school,

I learn to read, write and count, then I'm an adolescent, then a teenager, then I get a job or go to college, then I get married and have kids, and I develop a career of some kind, and I watch football on Saturdays and go to church on Sundays, then I get old, retire and then I die, hoping for the best after that."

But so often we don't stop and ask, "Why?"

- Who am I?
- Why am I here?
- What is my purpose in living?
- What is my purpose as a Christian?
- What has God called me to do?

If you don't know what your purpose is, you may miss it. You may spend your life on a multitude of things that will clutter up your time, but never fulfill God's purpose for your life.

We can be very busy in our lives without having a clear purpose in what we're doing.

> *Many are the plans in a man's heart, but it is the Lord's purpose that prevails. (Prov. 19:21)*

You only have one life. You only have one opportunity to do God's will and bring Him glory. Your life is as the flower in the field (Jam. 1:10-11). It's here today and then it's gone. So you need to know what God's purpose for you is, and then live your life with that purpose in mind.

You can know your purpose in life. God wants you to know what your purpose is. He's not hiding it from you.

Jesus was a Man who was led by purpose. Jesus knew who He was, and He knew what He was supposed to do.

> *He went to Nazareth, where he had been brought up, and on the Sabbath day he went into the synagogue, as was his custom. And he*

stood up to read. The scroll of the prophet Isaiah was handed to him. Unrolling it, he found the place where it is written: "The Spirit of the Lord is on me, because he has anointed me to preach good news to the poor. He has sent me to proclaim freedom for the prisoners and recovery of sight for the blind, to release the oppressed, to proclaim the year of the Lord's favor." Then he rolled up the scroll, gave it back to the attendant and sat down. The eyes of everyone in the synagogue were fastened on him, and he began by saying to them, "Today this scripture is fulfilled in your hearing." (Luke 4:16-21)

Jesus clearly knew what His purpose was. Consequently, at the end of His ministry, He was able to say to His Father:

I have brought you glory on earth by completing the work you gave me to do. (John 17:4)

At the end of his life, Paul could also write:

I am already being poured out like a drink offering, and the time has come for my departure. I have fought the good fight, I have finished the race, I have kept the faith. (2 Tim. 4:6-7)

This should be our goal at the end of our lives: to be able to say that we have fulfilled our purpose, not merely to have done some "good" things.

We Need Purpose in Our Churches

We also need to know our purpose as a church. We need to know our corporate purpose in God. Until we know the reason for which our church exists, we have no foundation, no motivation, and no direction or focus for ministry.

A church consultant did a survey and asked the members of nearly a thousand churches the question: "Why does the church exist?" Of the church members surveyed:

89% said, "The church's purpose is to take care of my family's and my needs."
11% said, "The purpose of the church is to win the world for Jesus Christ."

Then the consultant asked the pastors of those same churches the very same question.

Of the pastors:

90% said the purpose of the church was to win the world.
10% said the church's purpose was to care for the needs of the members.

The answers of the pastors were almost exactly the opposite of the answers of the church members! So is it any wonder that there is so much confusion, disagreement, and division within churches when the leaders and the people don't agree on why the church even exists.

However, there are some great benefits when there is a clear sense of purpose in a local church:

1.   A clear purpose builds strength.

Without a clear purpose for your life, you are weak. You meander in life, wandering from this to that, with no passion, no motivation, no conviction and no strength.

Corporately, when the guiding vision or purpose for a church is weak or has died, then that church dies, too. It degenerates into parties and camps, and eventually it falls apart.

However, the opposite is just as true: when there is a strong and clear vision in a local church, the people are disciplined and focused. They work together with energy and unity.

I appeal to you, brothers, in the name of our Lord Jesus Christ, that all of you agree with one another so that there may be no divisions among you and that you may be perfectly united in mind and thought. (1 Cor. 1:10)

Paul is not only writing about unity of doctrine in 1 Corinthians 1:10, but his primary meaning is unity of purpose. When we have unity of purpose, we will have harmony, peace, oneness of mind and a high level of morale. One brother said: When you're helping row the boat, you don't have time to rock it (cf. Eccl. 5:20)!

Which Church Will Be Stronger?

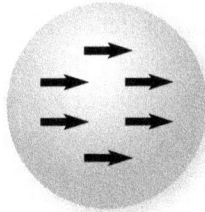

Church A	Church B
Unity of Purpose	Many Purposes

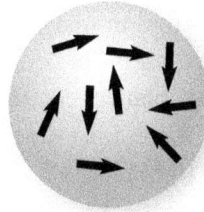

Thus, clear purpose builds strong people and strong churches. This is one of the main roles of leadership: to establish clear vision and unified direction.

2. A clear purpose reduces frustration.

There are both negative and positive sides to purpose. Purpose tells us not only what we should do, but also what we should not do. Therefore, we can focus on and accomplish what we are called to do, leaving the rest to whoever is called to do it.

Many people do not fail because they try to do too little, but because they try to do too much!

Each individual believer and each local church is not called to do everything. The world-wide universal church of Jesus Christ is called to do everything, but individual Christians and churches are not. Our calling is not to do it all. There is a difference between what God expects of His church and what God expects of one local congregation or one individual believer.

Each local church has a distinctive part of the total responsibility of the whole church, but God doesn't expect us to do it all. Jesus commanded the whole church to disciple all nations (Matt. 28:19); obviously each individual church cannot go to every nation!

Some think that God does expect them to do it all. A common idea found in many congregations, or denominations, is that "our congregation" or "our denomination" is God's only resource here on this planet – or at least His preeminent resource! The idea is that "if we don't do it, it probably won't get done, or at least get done right..."

Of course, this is not true. Each church has only a small part to play in God's overall purpose.

The same thing applies to you individually. You are not the only believer on the earth. God hasn't called you to be it all or to do it all. God has called you to do one little bit, and you should leave the rest to someone else.

The secret to effectiveness is to know what really counts, and then to do what really counts for you, and not to worry about the rest, however noble it all may be.

Each local church should not merely look for good things for churches to do, or for what worked well for someone else. We should look for how best to fulfill our own purpose and calling in God.

In addition, everything we do needs to fit our purpose. The ministries of our churches should not merely be random good ideas that we picked up from someone else. But they should all be a part of a conscious, deliberate, Holy Spirit-inspired plan to fulfill our purpose.

This means we must clearly know what our purpose is. Not having a clear purpose in your life is like driving a car along the highway without having a destination. Unfortunately, many churches are like that, and many people live their lives like that. They just, as it were, get in the car and start driving down the road. Then someone gets an impulse that they should turn here, and so they veer off in that direction, then someone else decides that it would be good to turn there, and so they swerve off in that direction. They constantly "fly by the seat of their pants," and half the time they go in circles. They may have a lot of fun in doing this, but they never really accomplish anything or get anywhere.

As Christians, we often have a great ability to spiritualize our disorganization or lack of purpose. We often justify that kind of personal lifestyle and church lifestyle as "being led by the Spirit." In reality, we are as "reeds shaken in the wind," "blown about by every wind of doctrine."

God is calling His people to know His will for their lives and to live to fulfill that will. God is not a hard taskmaster; each of us can fulfill His will. But, when we try to do it all, we get frustrated. We can't do it all. So we must focus on fulfilling our own purpose in God and not worry about the rest, but leave that to others. Thus, a clear purpose reduces frustration.

3.   A clear purpose allows cooperation.

Churches should not be mere collections of ministries bundled together. Our goal should be cooperation and integration. Our goal should be that all the ministries of the church fit together – that they all have the same purpose, the same vision, the same goal.

They should all be underpinned by the same motivation. They should all act according to the same set of values. They should seek to accomplish the same set of goals in the end.

From him the whole body, joined and held together by every supporting ligament, grows and builds itself up in love, as each part does its work. (Eph. 4:16)

The church is a living organism, composed of members vitally united to each other, each member with his own place and function, each essential to the body's health, each dependent on the rest of the body for its life and well-being, while the whole organism and all the individual members derive their life from the Head and act under His guidance.

Moreover, your life should be the same way. You should spend time reflecting on your life to see how God wants to put it all together. God will show you how to integrate all the aspects of your life to make it work as a unified whole. God does not want your family life to be divorced from your personal life, from your work life, or from your church life.

God wants our lives and our churches to be integrated so that all the various aspects and facets work together instead of competing against each other as separate, isolated identities with completely different, often conflicting, agendas.

As individuals, and as churches, we should seek one integrated identity. We want all our parts to be working together, moving in the same direction, and having the same purpose.

4. A clear purpose allows concentration.

The light of the sun will warm the surface of a dry leaf that is on the ground. But if you focus that light through a magnifying glass you will set the leaf on fire. Moreover, if you concentrate even more using a laser beam, you will be able to cut through a block of steel.

As we focus our energies – individually and as a church – we will have considerably more energy and a greater impact.

This was Paul's attitude. Paul focused on God's purposes:

> *Brothers, I do not consider myself yet to have taken hold of it. But one thing I do: Forgetting what is behind and straining toward what is ahead, I press on toward the goal to win the prize for which God has called me heavenward in Christ Jesus. (Phil. 3:13-14)*

Jesus also focused on the purposes of God:

> *I offered my back to those who beat me, my cheeks to those who pulled out my beard; I did not hide my face from mocking and spitting. Because the Sovereign Lord helps me, I will not be disgraced. Therefore have I set my face like flint, and I know I will not be put to shame. (Is. 50:6-7)*

The more we allow our energies to be diffused, the less success we will have in fulfilling God's will.

It is better to be excellent at a few things than mediocre at many. However, unless we know what our purpose is, we will not know where to concentrate. Thus, having a clear purpose allows us to concentrate.

As many have said, "The main thing is to keep the main thing the main thing."

There is a profound difference between efficiency and effectiveness. Efficiency is doing things right. Effectiveness is doing the right things. We do want to be efficient, but we want primarily to be effective.

Some lives and some churches are very well organized, but they do not accomplish very much of value.

Efficiency is not an end in itself. It should only be a means to the greater goal of effectiveness: to do the right things, and not to waste our energy and time on trivial things.

Many Christians live their lives as if they were arranging the deck chairs on the Titanic. Everything looks nice and very well organized, but the ship is sinking!

We need to keep our priorities straight and our lives and churches focused. We need to do the right things. We should do them well, but excellence for its own sake should not be our goal. Doing the precise will of God for our lives should be our goal.

5.   A clear purpose assists evaluation.

God tells us to evaluate ourselves:

> *Examine yourselves to see whether you are in the faith; test yourselves. Do you not realize that Christ Jesus is in you – unless, of course, you fail the test? (2 Cor. 13:5)*

Just how do we evaluate our lives and our churches? We certainly do not do it by comparing ourselves with others. We should evaluate our lives by asking:

- What has God called us to do?
- What is our purpose?
- How well are we accomplishing our purpose?

An honest evaluation of our lives and of our churches is only possible if we have first established a clear purpose.

In the remainder of this book we will discuss:

- Two principles of purpose:

    1. Your purpose is found in the will of God.
    2. Your purpose is found in the pursuit of God.

- Six specific paths to the discernment of purpose:

    1. You discern God's purpose through the Word of God.
    2. You discern God's purpose through the thoughts of your mind.
    3. You discern God's purpose through the inner witness in your heart by His Spirit.
    4. You discern God's purpose through prophetic revelation from God.
    5. You discern God's purpose through the counsel of others.
    6. You discern God's purpose through understanding your life's experiences.

Chapter 2

Your Purpose is Found in the Will of God

Many Christians ask pastors, "How do I find my place in the church? Where do I fit and how do I find that place?"

There is a related question that is not asked as often (perhaps it should be) and that is, "How do I discover my purpose in life?"

There are two overarching principles that will help you discern your purpose in life:

- Your purpose is found in the will of God.
- Your purpose is found in the pursuit of God.

Obedience to the will of God and the pursuit of God Himself are the proper contexts for discerning the purpose of God.

They are the necessary conditions that must be met first, or else the six paths to the discernment of God's purpose will not work. It is a waste of time to seek to know God's will unless you are prepared to submit to His will and unless you are seeking to know Him above everything else.

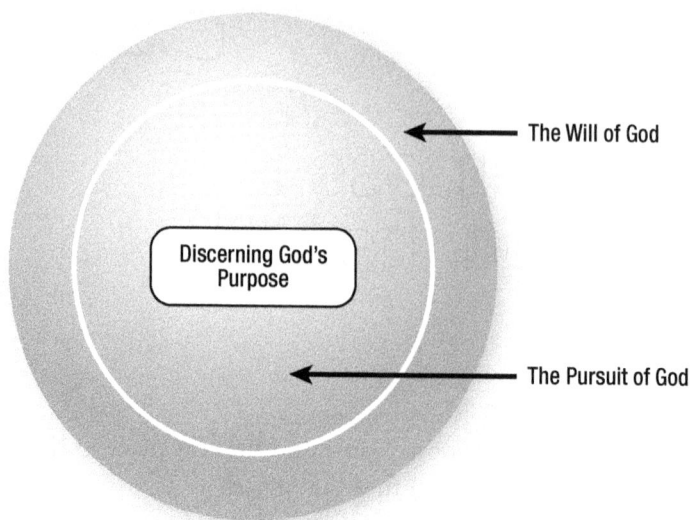

The Will of God

Discerning God's Purpose

The Pursuit of God

Principle 1: Your Purpose is Found in the Will of God

(God) has saved us and called us to a holy life – not because of anything we have done but because of his own purpose and grace... (2 Tim. 1:9)

God saved you according to His own purpose – not yours. So, in considering our purpose, this must be our first question: "Lord, what is the purpose you have given me?"

The question is not: "What do I want to accomplish in MY life?" The question is rather: "How does God want me to glorify Him in my life?"

Therefore do not be foolish, but understand what the Lord's will is. (Eph. 5:17)

God's purpose will be understood by those whose first desire is to know God's will and obey Him.

Many times we struggle with this. We ask God what His will is, and yet in our hearts we have not yet completely determined that we will obey Him if He asks us to do something we don't want to do.

Thus, the revelation of His purpose for us comes at the "sacrificial altar" where we surrender our lives to God:

> Therefore, I urge you, brothers, in view of God's mercy, to offer your bodies as living sacrifices, holy and pleasing to God – this is your spiritual act of worship. Do not conform any longer to the pattern of this world, but be transformed by the renewing of your mind. Then you will be able to test and approve what God's will is – his good, pleasing and perfect will. (Rom. 12:1-2)

It is as we present our lives to God as living sacrifices that we will understand His purpose. It is as we wrestle with our own wills and our own selfish purposes, and as God breaks us and crucifies us, making us like the Lord Jesus, bringing our wills into surrender to His, that we put ourselves in the place where God can fulfill His purpose through us (cf. Gen. 32:24-32).

Furthermore, God's plan is not just that He shows us what His will for us is and then we go off and struggle to do it in our own strength and by our own wisdom. God's way is through union with Jesus in His death and resurrection. In union with Jesus, His purpose truly becomes our purpose, and His life, strength and wisdom truly become our life, strength and wisdom. Then we will fulfill His purpose in His way, by His grace, in His strength, for His glory. That is what God wants.

Therefore, the purpose of God is a painful thing. It is not a pretty thing. It involves crucifixion and death. Fulfillment of His purpose comes through death: death to our own goals, our own ambitions, our own purposes, our own wisdom and strength.

The purpose of God is not found in a big public meeting when a world famous prophet calls you out in front of everyone and tells you that you're a great person and that you've got a spectacular calling and that the whole world is going to notice you and adore you. But the purpose of God is found in the quietness of your own inner life, in the pain of your own wrestling and agonizing with God as He deals with you at the center of your being and your will. The purpose of God is found as He deals with you about lordship, as He deals with you about the central issue of who will really be the Lord and God of your life.

When you were saved, you received a whole Lord Jesus Christ – an entire Lord Jesus. He gave Himself for you, holding nothing back, and He gave Himself to you completely and without reservation. When you fully surrender to the Lord Jesus, He receives a whole you. That is what He wants. Furthermore, that is all He will accept.

In taxation, the government asks us for a percentage of our income. But Jesus demands the entirety of our lives: all we are, all we have, all we ever will be.

He gave Himself completely to you. He requires that you give yourself completely to Him, as a living sacrifice.

The emblem of the Moravian missionaries was an altar and a yoke, with an ox standing between them. Underneath are the Latin words for, "Ready for either." We are the ox between the yoke and the sacrifice. The choice is God's. From our side, we must choose to be "ready for either." We must be ready to die for God if He so chooses; we must be ready to live a life of service for God if that's what He wants.

When Jesus redeemed you, He purchased you. He didn't just purchase your freedom from sin and eternal destruction; He purchased you.

> Do you not know that your body is a temple of the Holy Spirit, who is in you, whom you have received from God? You are not your own; you were bought at a price. Therefore honor God with your body. (1 Cor. 6:19-20)

God purchased you – all of you – and He did it once and for all. He has already purchased every aspect of your life. He owns your life, but

He still wants you to lay it on the altar by an act of your will. He still wants you to bring it to Him, to give it to Him, keeping nothing back for yourself.

One young Native American man was at a Christian meeting. He saw people going up to the altar. He realized God was calling him to give everything to Him. First he offered his blanket, then his jewelry, and then his horse. Finally, he realized God didn't want things, God wanted him. So he went up and offered himself to God, laying himself on the altar. That is the gospel!

Many times we give to the Lord those parts of our lives that we really don't want anyway. Modern evangelism doesn't help in this regard. We tell people: "Come to Jesus, give Him your pain, give Him your hurts, give Him your sin." But that's not what the gospel of the Kingdom is. The message of the Kingdom is: God demands you – not just your hurts or pains, or your debts, but you. Not just the things you don't want anyway, but the things you do want: give it all to Him. Give yourself to Him.

Sometimes people – whose lives are in a mess – get saved when we tell them to give their hurts to Jesus. However, as soon as things in their lives look a little better, they turn around and take their lives back again, and we wonder why. But we weren't honest with them in the first place. The gospel is Jesus' demand for all of you in response to His gift to you of all of Him. Jesus gave all of Himself for you and to you, that you may give all of yourself to Him.

Only you can do that – only you can make that decision. No one else can get married for you, and no one else can become a fully surrendered Christian for you.

We all must wrestle for ourselves. We all must answer the question for ourselves: who will we serve – ourselves or God? Who will we truly make the Lord of our lives? Not just the Lord of our pain and the Lord of the things we don't want, but Lord of all.

Enemies of Surrender to God

Here are some of the reasons we do not surrender ourselves to God:

1.   Spiritual laziness.

All of this seems like such hard work – surrendering to God in the first place, and then serving Him with abandon for the rest of your life. Many people want to get away with the bare minimum of Christian experience. They want to somehow make it into God's kingdom in the end. They want somehow to scrape through life just being saved in the end, but without getting too radical in the meantime. Such spiritual laziness is the mortal enemy of the purpose of God in your life.

2.   Complacency.

This is the attitude of: "Why do I need to be surrendered? I'm getting along pretty well by myself. Why do I need to give myself to Jesus?"

In America, self-sufficiency is one of our greatest problems. In a time of peace and great prosperity, we're doing fine without God. Even in our churches, we're doing fine without God! Many churches carry on with their own programs and agendas and plans. It all looks pious, but God is not in it. It's like the whirlwind outside of Elijah's cave: a tremendous amount of noise and fuss, but God isn't in it. Sometimes we may wonder if we in America even know or care whether or not God is with us and in what we do, because we can make it work so well without Him.

3.   Bad examples.

Some Christians declare their life to be one of surrender and obedience to God and yet they are either incredibly boring and dull, or they are off on some weird, unbalanced tangent. Understandably, other Christians don't want to be like them. Nevertheless, God is not boring, and neither is He weird and unbalanced.

Moreover, people who are boring or weird are usually not surrendered to God, anyway. They're usually following their own purposes and agendas; they just know how to say the right things.

In any case, God is not going to put you in someone else's mold. You have unique fingerprints. God has only made one like you (thank God!) and, fully surrendered to the Lord Jesus, you will be the person that God wants you to be.

So, do not try to imitate someone else in any way. Follow the Lord Jesus and be what He wants you to be.

4. Suspicion.

Some Christians are suspicious of God. They suspect that He will take advantage of them in some way, if they give Him absolutely everything. What a foolish thought! God loves you more than you love yourself. He's not going to take advantage of you. He's not going to use you or abuse you.

Some people are afraid that if they surrender fully to God, then He might send them somewhere they don't want to go. Well, maybe He will. But if that's what He wants for you, then you'll be far happier in your new location in the middle of His purpose, than you will be anywhere else, out of God's purpose.

God is wiser than you are. His ways and purposes are better than yours!

5. Fear of unfulfillment.

Some are afraid that a secret hope will be unfulfilled. They are afraid that if they give themselves to God they will not be able to do something that they really want to do.

Certainly, there may be some secret sin you want to try that God won't let you do. Or perhaps there is some ambition in your heart, and you're not sure God shares it. But, whatever God does have for you will be better – far, far better – than whatever ideas you have for yourself. Furthermore, when you surrender yourself to God, He takes the desire for those other things out of your heart anyway.

6.   Fear of failure.

Some are afraid that if they surrender to God, they will not be able to keep it up. They think that it will be too hard for them. But God will help you fulfill His purpose.

> To him who is able to keep you from falling and to present you before his glorious presence without fault and with great joy – to the only God our Savior be glory, majesty, power and authority, through Jesus Christ our Lord, before all ages, now and forevermore! Amen. (Jude 24-25)

God has the power to guide you; He has the power to keep you. Your failure in the past has not been because you were surrendered to God; it was because you weren't!

7.   The sins of the past.

For some people, the sins and failures of the past keep them from God now.

However, when Jesus forgives, He also forgets. Our sins and failures of the past are as far from us as the east is from the west:

> For as high as the heavens are above the earth, so great is his love for those who fear him; as far as the east is from the west, so far

has he removed our transgressions from us. (Ps. 103:11-12)

…You have lovingly delivered my soul from the pit of corruption, For You have cast all my sins behind Your back. (Is. 38:17, NKJV)

One woman had a vision of the Lord Jesus. He stood at the bottom of her bed, holding a bundle of filthy rags, representing her sins. As she watched, He took the bundle and cast it behind His back. The wall behind Him opened and the bundle hurtled through a long tunnel into eternity. It got smaller and smaller until it finally disappeared – her sins were gone, cast behind God's back!

Sometimes people don't let the past go because they carry guilt around. If God has forgiven us, we should let the past go and get on with our purpose in God!

Full Surrender

What does full surrender mean?

It means, firstly, that you give to the Lord Jesus as much of yourself as you know of yourself, and then the rest that you don't know. There are vast areas of your will, your understanding, your emotions, and your affections that you don't know.

My conscience is clear, but that does not make me innocent. It is the Lord who judges me. (1 Cor. 4:4)

…God is greater than our hearts, and he knows everything. (1 John 3:20)

So bundle it all together – all you know of yourself – and all you don't know of yourself – and lay it once and for all in His hand.

Secondly, purpose to do that daily. Purpose to do it minute by minute: to continually hand over the lordship of your heart and life to Him. Once is not enough; you need to do it each and every day.

This daily, ongoing submission to God will have a significant practical impact on the decisions you make. In all your decisions, you should humbly submit, in advance, to the outworking of God's sovereign will as it touches your every decision:

> Now listen, you who say, "Today or tomorrow we will go to this or that city, spend a year there, carry on business and make money." Why, you do not even know what will happen tomorrow. What is your life? You are a mist that appears for a little while and then vanishes. Instead, you ought to say, "If it is the Lord's will, we will live and do this or that." (Jam. 4:13-15)

If you do not surrender to God daily, your initial surrender to God will become some past memory getting sadder and sadder as the years go by.

Give all your purposes, ambitions, desires, motives, agendas and activities to Him. Give him your mind, your thoughts and your imaginations. He owns it all anyway. Your thoughts are not just your private possessions. They are His. He has purchased the rightful ownership of them with His own blood. So, give them to Him, day by day, hour by hour, minute by minute.

Chapter 3

Your Purpose is Found in the Pursuit of God

As we have seen, our purpose is found in God – in His will. So we must daily seek heart surrender to Him and to His plan in order to know His purpose. We don't want to pursue our purpose at all; we want to pursue His purpose for us.

Our purpose is found in the will of God. Yet the will of God for each of our lives differs quite a bit at many points. He calls one to do this, He calls another to do that. There can be a lot of difference in our divine callings and purposes.

Nevertheless, there is one calling that God has given to each of us. That calling is expressed in a variety of ways in our lives, but the calling itself is the same for all us. That calling is found in John 17:3.

> *Now this is eternal life: that they may know you, the only true God, and Jesus Christ, whom you have sent. (John 17:3)*

> *God, who has called you into fellowship with his Son Jesus Christ our Lord, is faithful. (1 Cor. 1:9)*

God's will is for all of us to know Him. Thus, before you can receive guidance from God, you must yourself be guided to God.

God's purpose for us is not merely to do things for Him, but to know Him. He calls us His "friends," not just His servants:

> I no longer call you servants, because a servant does not know his master's business. Instead, I have called you friends, for everything that I learned from my Father I have made known to you. (John 15:15)

This is our second principle.

Principle 2: Your Purpose is Found in the Pursuit of God

Your purpose is found in the pursuit of God Himself. Your purpose is found in knowing God.

Paul spoke of the Lord Jesus in his letter to the Colossian believers:

> ...in everything he might have the supremacy. (Col. 1:18)

Jesus has the supremacy in all. He, Himself, is preeminent in all.

When Paul writes in his letters about his own life and experiences, sooner or later he always comes to the subject of the Lord Jesus: of His greatness, of His beauty, of His glory, of His all-sufficiency, and of our high calling to union with Him. Paul was a man who was absorbed with the Lord Jesus. He was a man who had made a wonderful discovery in his life. He had discovered the meaning of all things, the purpose of all things. Paul had discovered the One who has the preeminence in all.

Paul was no spiritual slouch before he found the Lord Jesus. Paul was not a hippie living on the beach, surfing all day and partying all night. He had been a devoutly religious man. Paul had spent his life seeking to know the law and to obey it with all his heart. Paul had spent his life trying to do the will of God. Paul had spent his life seeking to fulfill the purpose of God.

Here is his testimony:

> *circumcised on the eighth day, of the people of Israel, of the tribe of Benjamin, a Hebrew of Hebrews; in regard to the law, a Pharisee; as for zeal, persecuting the church; as for legalistic righteousness, faultless. But whatever was to my profit I now consider loss for the sake of Christ. What is more, I consider everything a loss compared to the surpassing greatness of knowing Christ Jesus my Lord, for whose sake I have lost all things. I consider them rubbish, that I may gain Christ (Phil. 3:5-8)*

Paul discovered the One who has the preeminence in all. From that moment on, Paul no longer pursued righteousness for its own sake, or obedience for its own sake or purpose for its own sake, but Paul pursued Him.

This is the highest life. This is the true Christian life.

> *Now this is eternal life: that they may know you, the only true God, and Jesus Christ, whom you have sent. (John 17:3)*

This is the purpose for everything in our lives: to know Him.

Our Purpose in Everything is to Know Him

According to the Scriptures, our purpose in everything is to know the Lord Jesus. We can see this in a number of ways.

1. The reason God gave us His Word was to bring us to the Person of Jesus.

In these days of intellectual sophistication, our Bible colleges and seminaries have often substituted a mental comprehension of the Scriptures for a heart-changing, personal experience of God. This is not something that is unique to our day, for the religiously orthodox of Jesus' day did the very same thing.

> *You diligently study the Scriptures because you think that by them you possess eternal life. These are the Scriptures that testify about me, yet you refuse to come to me to have life. (John 5:39-40)*

Those religious leaders knew the Word – at least superficially. Yet Jesus rebuked them. Even though they presented themselves as great scholars of the Scriptures, they rejected Him who was the entire subject and purpose of those very Scriptures. They rejected the One who is the embodiment of the Scriptures, the One who has the preeminence in all.

The purpose of the Word of God is to bring us into greater fellowship with Jesus; to personally know Him in a greater way; to find intimate union with Him. Certainly, we should engage ourselves in theology, and in disciplined, rigorous study of the Word of God. But the ultimate purpose of it all is to know Him.

> *We know also that the Son of God has come and has given us understanding, so that we may know him who is true... (1 John 5:20)*

Are you seeking knowledge and understanding? Jesus is the Truth (John 14:6). You can never come to any knowledge of Truth apart from knowing Him. In Him personally, in His Person, in Him "are hidden all the treasures of wisdom and knowledge" (Col. 2:3). Only through the apprehension of Jesus will these treasures ever be revealed.

2. **Our obedience is not an end in itself,
   but it is a means to a greater end.**

The purpose of obedience is Him: to experience Him – His glorious presence directly in our lives, His power and majesty, and His overwhelming love and grace.

> *Whoever has my commands and obeys them, he is the one who loves me. He who loves me will be loved by my Father, and I too will love him and show myself to him…If anyone loves me, he will obey my teaching. My Father will love him, and we will come to him and make our home with him. (John 14:21-23)*

Our obedience to God brings us into fellowship with the Lord Jesus. That is our purpose – knowing Him.

3. **The reason we endure sufferings in this life
   is to find Jesus in a greater way.**

The purpose of our sufferings is Him.

> *What is more, I consider everything a loss compared to the surpassing greatness of knowing Christ Jesus my Lord, for whose sake I have lost all things. I consider them rubbish, that I may gain Christ…I want to know Christ and the power of his resurrection and the fellowship of sharing in his sufferings, becoming like him in his death, (Phil. 3:8-10)*

Our sufferings bring us into greater fellowship with Jesus. God will offer us only one path by which we can enter into the true knowledge of Jesus: the fellowship of His cross.

It is easy to say we love God for Himself when everything is going well. But what if it will cost us everything – our own goals and ambitions and comforts, even our own lives – to serve Him? Will we still love Him for His own sake?

Sufferings purify our love for Him and bring us into a higher place of fellowship and union with Him.

Suffering itself doesn't help you. In fact, sufferings destroy many Christians. They become bitter and angry. Their heart grows hard against God. Other believers, however, respond to suffering by falling with brokenness upon the grace of God. Sufferings help them to mature in Christ.

> He who falls on this stone will be broken to pieces, but he on whom it falls will be crushed. (Matt. 21:44)

Suffering does not, by itself, cause you to grow in God, but it gives you the opportunity to grow in God. God's intention in allowing suffering in your life is that you abandon all hope and trust in your own strength, and in your own ways, and in the things of this life to sustain you, and throw yourself more completely upon Jesus and His wonderful grace.

If you will do that, if you will submit yourself to God and rejoice through the pain He allows to come your way, knowing it is all for your greater participation in His glory, then you will have learned the meaning of your life upon the earth.

> ...when he has tested me, I will come forth as gold. (Job 23:10)

> For our light and momentary troubles are achieving for us an eternal glory that far outweighs them all. So we fix our eyes not on what is seen, but on what is unseen. For what is seen is temporary, but what is unseen is eternal. (2 Cor. 4:17-18)

Jesus has the preeminence in all.

> I want to know Christ and the power of his resurrection and the fellowship of sharing in his sufferings, becoming like him in his death, (Phil. 3:10)

4.   The reason God has set us in the local church
is to find Jesus in a greater way.

The purpose of church life is Jesus. Separately we each have only a "piece" of the one loaf – representing Himself – that Jesus broke and distributed among His disciples (Luke 22:19). It is together in the Body of Christ that we find Him in all His fullness:

> *built on the foundation of the apostles and prophets, with Christ Jesus himself as the chief cornerstone. In him the whole building is joined together and rises to become a holy temple in the Lord. And in him you too are being built together to become a dwelling in which God lives by his Spirit. (Eph. 2:20-22)*

> *so that Christ may dwell in your hearts through faith. And I pray that you, being rooted and established in love, may have power, together with all the saints, to grasp how wide and long and high and deep is the love of Christ, and to know this love that surpasses knowledge – that you may be filled to the measure of all the fullness of God. (Eph. 3:17-19)*

> *Instead, speaking the truth in love, we will in all things grow up into him who is the Head, that is, Christ. (Eph. 4:15; cf. vv. 11-16)*

That is why we must forgive one another and serve one another. That is why we must work on bearing each other's burdens. That is why each of us must be a committed, vital and participating part of the local church where God has set us: because Jesus has the preeminence in all, because He is our purpose.

All we do in this life is for that end: to know Him in a greater way.

The purpose of everything is Jesus, and the purpose of everything in your life should be Him: to know Him, to be united with Him in His love, His grace and His glory. When that is your vision, when that becomes your highest over-riding, all-encompassing purpose, you will be changed. Then you will be holy, and you will be righteous, and you will be obedient, and you will win souls, and you will grow and mature as a believer, and you will do all those good and proper things that we so often try to do apart from Him.

When He – He Himself – has the preeminence in all of your life, then you will be changed.

> *And we, who with unveiled faces all reflect the Lord's glory, are being transformed into his likeness with ever-increasing glory, which comes from the Lord, who is the Spirit. (2 Cor. 3:18)*

We will always have temptations; but the reason we have struggles with temptations in our hearts, and the reason we occasionally fail, is because Jesus is not yet in a place of preeminence in all. The reason the world looks so attractive sometimes (when we know it's nothing but death) is because He is not yet in a place of preeminence in all. The reason we get frustrated with each other in the church sometimes is because He is not yet in a place of preeminence in all. The reason we kick and whine when things don't go our way all the time in our lives is because He is not yet in a place of preeminence in all. The reason we don't bear the fruit we know we should bear is because He is not yet in a place of preeminence in all.

But in your heart, you want Him to be preeminent in all. Deep in your heart, there is a cry. It's a cry for God. It's a cry to know God. It's a cry to reach out to God. It's a cry to see God, to touch God.

Before the world began, there was only God: God was all in all. In 1 Corinthians 15:28, Paul says the time is coming when all things will be subdued under the Lord Jesus, and then the Son of God Himself also will be subject to Him that put all things under Him, that God may be all in all.

That is what you were made for. That is what is in your heart, now, as a born again believer. God has put this in your heart. He's called you to know Him. He's called you to give Jesus the preeminence in all. He already has the preeminence in all. But He asks you to put Him first in your life and in your heart. He calls you to seek Him first, to give Him the preeminence.

> *O God, You are my God; Early will I seek You; My soul thirsts for You; My flesh longs for You In a dry and thirsty land Where there is no water. So I have looked for You in the sanctuary, To see Your power and Your glory. (Ps. 63:1-2, NKJV)*

> *As the deer pants for the water brooks, So pants my soul for You, O God. My soul thirsts for God, for the living God. When shall I come and appear before God? (Ps. 42:1-2, NKJV)*

He is your purpose. All the other principles of purpose are useless if they are not based upon surrender to God and pursuit of Him first of all.

Chapter 4

Discerning God's Purpose

Our discernment of God's will is entirely dependent upon the work of the Holy Spirit.

> *But when he, the Spirit of truth, comes, he will guide you into all truth. He will not speak on his own; he will speak only what he hears, and he will tell you what is yet to come. (John 16:13)*

> *However, as it is written: "No eye has seen, no ear has heard, no mind has conceived what God has prepared for those who love him" – but God has revealed it to us by his Spirit. The Spirit searches all things, even the deep things of God. For who among men knows the thoughts of a man except the man's spirit within him? In the same way no one knows the thoughts of God except the Spirit of God. We have not received the spirit of the world but the Spirit who is from God, that we may understand what God has freely given us. (1 Cor. 2:9-12)*

The Holy Spirit illuminates God's purpose to us. Moreover, He does this in conjunction with prayer.

> *If any of you lacks wisdom, he should ask God, who gives generously to all without finding fault, and it will be given to him. (Jam. 1:5)*

Thus, prayer and dependency on the work of the Holy Spirit are the foundation on which we build our knowledge of God's purpose.

This knowledge of God's purpose is built in six ways. These are the six major ways to discern God's will for your life; whether it's His purpose for your life overall, or His will concerning some particular issue or decision you're facing.

In a life of prayer, we discern the will of God, through the illumination of the Holy Spirit, by:

1. The Word of God.
2. The thoughts of your mind.
3. The inner witness in your heart by His Spirit.
4. Prophetic revelation from God.
5. The counsel of others.
6. Understanding your life's experiences.

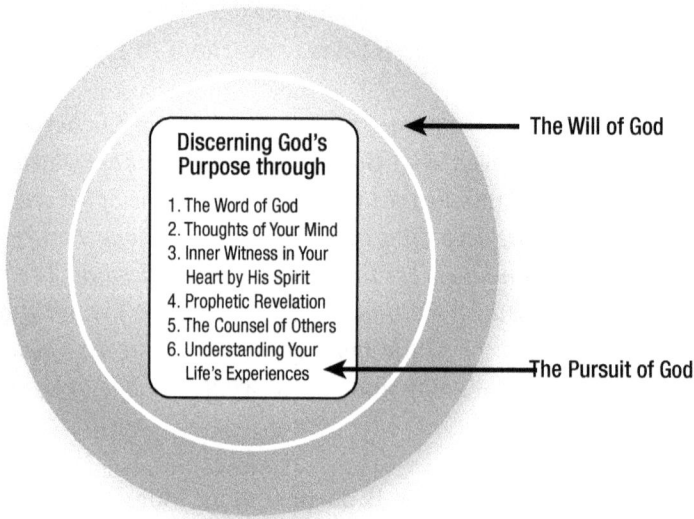

Discerning God's
Purpose through

1. The Word of God
2. Thoughts of Your Mind
3. Inner Witness in Your
   Heart by His Spirit
4. Prophetic Revelation
5. The Counsel of Others
6. Understanding Your
   Life's Experiences

The Will of God

The Pursuit of God

These six ways work together to give you an overall conviction regarding God's will. Many times there will be much overlap between them. For example, the counsel of others may witness to your heart that the matter you are considering is God's will. Prophetic revelation may point to particular passages of Scripture as applicable in a situation.

A wise strategy is to consider all six ways when seeking to understand God's overall purpose for your life, and, as much as possible, to have all six in agreement before making a major decision.

Chapter 5

You Discern God's Purpose Through the Word of God

The first path to discern God's will is through His Word.

A great deal of God's purpose for your life has already been revealed in the Word of God. He has given you 66 books filled with wisdom and filled with the revelation of His will in one form or another.

Therefore, God's purpose will be shown to those who diligently study and meditate on the Word of God.

After Romans 12:1 (surrender to God) comes Romans 12:2.

> *Do not conform any longer to the pattern of this world, but be transformed by the renewing of your mind. Then you will be able to test and approve what God's will is – his good, pleasing and perfect will. (Rom. 12:2)*

As you are transformed through the Word of God, you will be able to fulfill God's will for your life. This is because you will find in the Word the specific answers and principles you need, and also because of the spiritual life that is in the Word of God.

For the word of God is living and powerful... (Heb. 4:12, NKJV)

The Word of God is living and powerful. The Word of God is so powerful, that God created the world by His Word:

> *By faith we understand that the universe was formed at God's command... (Heb. 11:3)*

God created the entire universe out of nothing, by His Word. Since that time, God continues to hold the whole universe together by His Word:

> *The Son is...sustaining all things by his powerful word... (Heb. 11:3)*

The word of God is powerful. Moreover, God's Word has spiritual life. Jesus said:

> *...The words I have spoken to you are spirit and they are life. (John 6:63)*

Paul wrote:

> *And we also thank God continually because, when you received the word of God, which you heard from us, you accepted it not as the word of men, but as it actually is, the word of God, which is at work in you who believe. (1 Thess. 2:13)*

The Word of God "is at work" in those who believe. The Word of God has the power to change your life; it actually possesses the power to do things in your life, as you get into the Word and the Word gets into you.

> *Like newborn babies, crave pure spiritual milk, so that by it you may grow up in your salvation, (1 Pet 2:2)*

We need the word of God to have spiritual life:

> *Jesus answered, "It is written: 'Man does not live on bread alone, but on every word that comes from the mouth of God.'" (Matt. 4:4)*

To the Ephesian elders, Paul said:

> *Now I commit you to God and to the word of his grace, which can build you up and give you an inheritance among all those who are sanctified. (Acts 20:32)*

The word of God is our food. The word of God is our spiritual meat. The Word is our life. It does not merely contain a future hope, but also the power now for wisdom, strength, joy, peace, life and victory. Through meditating in the Word, you will grow spiritually strong, and you will be more sensitive to the Holy Spirit leading and guiding you. You'll grow in wisdom and be more perceptive to the hand of God in your circumstances. Overall, you will find it easier to discern and understand God's purpose for your life. In Matthew 7:13-27, Jesus gives a series of examples, and in all of them, the Word of God makes the difference between success and failure.

The Importance of the Word of God

Our lives should revolve around the Scriptures. We should be people who place a great priority on knowing the Word and on obeying it.

God reveals His will and purpose to us through His Word.

> *Do your best to present yourself to God as one approved, a workman who does not need to be ashamed and who correctly handles the word of truth. (2 Tim. 2:15)*

The Word of God is not just academic. It is your life. Your life, your growth as a Christian, your future, and whether or not you fulfill your purpose revolves around your life in the Word. The Word of God is not just for preachers to know, or for students in seminaries to study, but it's for all of us daily to meditate in and to apply to our lives.

In the Scriptures, it is said that those who attend to the Word hold fast to the Lord and to eternal life,

> *Watch your life and doctrine closely. Persevere in them, because if you do, you will save both yourself and your hearers. (1 Tim. 4:16)*

There are many churches who are very supportive of the Holy Spirit's work in the life of the believer, but who are unbalanced, having come to the point where "doctrine" is looked down on. "Doctrine" is seen as something that the "denominations" were involved in. (As if anything that the "denominations" are involved in is to be avoided!)

For many, this has become a convenient way out of a lot of work. Their belief is that they don't need to study the Scriptures because they "hear from the Lord." Study is just for people without the Holy Spirit!

However, God says:

> *Watch your life and doctrine closely. Persevere in them, because if you do, you will save both yourself and your hearers. (1 Tim. 4:16)*

Paul (who wrote these words), of course, had the Holy Spirit, and Timothy (to whom Paul wrote these words) did, too!

There is great deal in the New Testament concerning the importance of knowing the Word and having correct doctrine:

> *Now, brothers, I want to remind you of the gospel I preached to you, which you received and on which you have taken your stand. By this gospel you are saved, if you hold firmly to the word I preached to you. Otherwise, you have believed in vain. (1 Cor. 15:1-2)*

> *Avoid godless chatter, because those who indulge in it will become more and more ungodly. Their teaching will spread like gangrene. Among them are Hymenaeus and Philetus, who have wandered away from the truth. They say that the resurrection has already*

taken place, and they destroy the faith of some. (2 Tim. 2:16-18)

...our dear brother Paul also wrote you with the wisdom that God gave him. He writes the same way in all his letters, speaking in them of these matters. His letters contain some things that are hard to understand, which ignorant and unstable people distort, as they do the other Scriptures, to their own destruction. Therefore, dear friends, since you already know this, be on your guard so that you may not be carried away by the error of lawless men and fall from your secure position. (2 Pet. 3:15-17)

This is why teachers of the Word of God will receive a stricter judgment (Jam. 3:1).

The church of God is called:

...the pillar (the Greek word means prop or support) *and foundation* (the Greek word means stay, undergirding; from the verb which means to make stable, settle firmly) *of the truth. (1 Tim. 3:15)*

We are commanded by God to seek doctrinal purity,

Do your best to present yourself to God as one approved, a workman who does not need to be ashamed and who correctly handles the word of truth. (2 Tim. 2:15)

and to keep the church free from error:

I urge you, brothers, to watch out for those who cause divisions and put obstacles in your way that are contrary to the teaching you have learned. Keep away from them. (Rom. 16:17)

Paul took correct doctrine very seriously. Moreover, Paul was not the only one. John, who wrote so beautifully concerning our fellowship with Jesus through His Spirit, also wrote some very strong words concerning true doctrine:

See that what you have heard from the beginning remains in you. If it does, you also will remain in the Son and in the Father. And this is what he promised us – even eternal life. (1 John 2:24-25)

Anyone who runs ahead and does not continue in the teaching of Christ does not have God; whoever continues in the teaching has both the Father and the Son. (2 John 9)

This was the very same John who wrote John 17:3. The Christian life is to know God, but if you don't have the right doctrine, you don't have God and you don't know God. That is what John wrote! There is no contradiction between knowing God and having good doctrine.

Levels of Authority of Doctrine

To have a proper balance, we must recognize that our doctrines have various levels of authority.

Jesus said there are certain doctrinal matters that are "more important" than others:

…you have neglected the more important matters of the law – justice, mercy and faithfulness… (Matt. 23:23)

By implication, this means there are some doctrinal matters that are "less important." We must realize that our doctrines have varying degrees of significance and of authority. They are not all equally important (although, of course, nothing in the Bible is unimportant).

Vital doctrines such as the deity of Christ, the substitutionary blood atonement, Jesus' virgin birth and bodily resurrection, justification by faith alone, the inerrancy of Scripture, the triunity of the Godhead, etc., that are clearly taught in the Scripture must never be compromised. These are the doctrines for which you should be prepared to die and which you should defend even if it means causing division in the local church.

However, issues such as the exact method of water baptism and, the timing of the rapture, forms of worship, method of taking communion, or the appropriateness of Christians observing Christmas should not be the causes of church divisions. You should be prepared to die for the deity of Christ, but not for someone's speculation regarding the meaning of Paul's head covering in 1 Corinthians 11![1] You should not divide churches over disagreements about the historical identity of the king called "Darius the Mede" in the Old Testament book of Daniel!

The following graphic shows the relationship between a particular doctrine's importance and clarity and its subsequent authority.

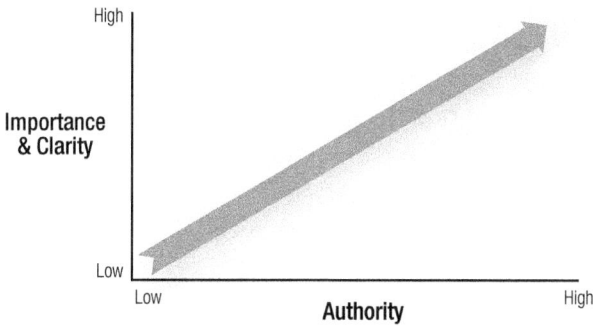

As the importance and clarity of the doctrine increases, its authority increases. However, if a doctrine is relatively less important or clear, then its authority decreases.

---

[1] In some of our Hispanic churches, the women sincerely believe they should wear the head covering during public meetings. We respect that genuine conviction on their part.

There are five levels of authority of doctrines[2]:

Level 1. Direct statements in Scripture. To the extent that our doctrines are built on direct statements and not on interpretations of Scripture, they have the highest level of authority. They are the direct, clear Word of God. There is no element of human interpretation involved. For example, the fact that Jesus is God is directly stated many times in the Bible:

> *In the beginning was the Word, and the Word was with God, and the Word was God. (John 1:1; cf. 20:28; Is. 9:6; Rom. 9:5; Tit. 2:13; 2 Pet. 1:1; Heb. 1:8-9; etc.)*

"Level 1" doctrines that are built simply on direct statements of Scripture are doctrines for which we can, and should, be willing to die. These are the doctrines we need to believe to be saved. If we disagree with these doctrines, we are not saved.

Other examples of direct statements are Jesus' genuine humanity (1 Tim. 2:5), His substitutionary blood atonement (Is. 53), His bodily resurrection (Luke 24:39), and justification by faith alone (Rom. 3:28).

Level 2. Direct implications of Scripture. These are "close interpretations" from the Scripture. They are interpretations, as opposed to direct statements, but they are very "close" interpretations, as opposed to "distant." Consequently, they are not quite as authoritative as direct statements, because there is an additional small step of interpretation involved. These doctrines, however, still carry a high level of authority and should be taken very seriously. An example of this kind of doctrine is the triune nature of God. There is no verse that explicitly says, "God is three in one," yet there is much clear scriptural evidence for this truth.

---

[2] To say there are exactly "five" levels of authority is arbitrary and has no biblical basis. The general idea of differing levels of authority of doctrines is, however, biblical. The designation of five levels used here helps us to grasp this valuable principle. For the sake of simplicity, it may sometimes be better to reduce the five levels to three: Dogma (Levels 1 & 2), Doctrine (Level 3), and Tradition or Speculation (Levels 4 & 5).

Level 3. Probable implications of Scripture. There is a much greater degree of interpretation involved in the formulation of these doctrines. The authority of these doctrines increases as the number of Scriptures used to support them increases (as long as those Scriptures are interpreted with accuracy and integrity). Level 3 doctrines often become the particular "distinctives" between one Christian group and the next. An example of such a doctrine would be the relationship of divine sovereignty to human responsibility. While many would argue this doctrine to be fairly clear from a study of the entire Bible, this is probably not a doctrine for which you should die. Another example of this level of doctrine is the method of water baptism that one uses or one's position on divorce and remarriage. We all should believe, teach and practice our differing convictions on these matters, but we should still be able to work together as believers as long as we agree on Level 1 and 2 doctrines.

Level 4. Inductive conclusions from Scripture. This is when we look at what the whole Bible says about something, seeking to understand it in the context of history and culture, trying to understand what the author originally intended by his words to those people in that place at that time, and prayerfully considering how to apply it to our lives now. There is quite a lot of interpretation entailed in these conclusions, and the more interpretation involved, the less authoritative the doctrine becomes. This doesn't automatically mean that such a doctrine is wrong, but it does mean that we shouldn't burn someone at the stake simply because he disagrees with it!

"Level 4" issues are addressed in the Scriptures in some form or another, but there is a high level of interpretation involved in these doctrines. Some examples are: one's particular view concerning the rapture, the correct mode of women's dress, the precise function of deacons, the role of women in the church, the meaning of the head-covering in 1 Corinthians 11, etc.

Many of our hallowed church traditions are actually "Level 4" doctrines. To some believers these doctrines are absolutely clear. However, in reality, they are not so clear. Problems arise when believers become dogmatic over "Level 4" doctrines, and many churches have been divided or destroyed over such issues.

Level 5. Speculations from Scripture. These doctrines are derived from a single statement or hint in the Scripture. Frequently they come from an obscure or unclear part of the Bible. They may also involve "spiritualization" of the Scriptures. These are theories; in fact, they are often guesses. In spite of the fact that doctrines of this nature frequently become very big issues in churches, nevertheless, in reality they possess little authority.

Here are some examples of these theories:

- Some say the distance of 2000 cubits between the Ark and the people in Joshua 3:4 represents the 2000 year period between Jesus' resurrection and that of His people at His return. Of course, this is pure spiritualization and speculation. The difficulty with this interpretation is further compounded by the fact that some Hebrew texts (along with modern translations) say 1000 cubits!
- Some teach that Gideon's Army in Judges 7 is a prophetic type of God's "end-time army" that consists of an elite group of believers. One cult in China has developed a large following with this teaching, and the leader claims to be Christ Himself!
- Others combine Peter's assertion that "with the Lord a day is like a thousand years, and a thousand years are like a day" (2 Pet. 3:8) with the six days of creation to suggest that there will be a total of only 6000 years of human history, before Christ returns to institute the Millennium – the "seventh day" of rest on the earth. This idea is nowhere found in the Scripture and is contradicted by the genealogies of Genesis,[3] which indicate a period of time somewhat longer than this, and also by the Early Church's belief that Christ would return in their generation (e.g., 1 Thess. 4:17). If one reads Psalm 90:4, from which Peter quoted, it is obvious that the "thousands years" is intended to be understood poeti-

---

[3] The difficulty of determining the exact time periods indicated by the genealogies in Genesis is compounded by the omission of links in them.

cally: "For a thousand years in your sight are like a day that has just gone by, or like a watch in the night."

- The "Gap theory" that says there was a "gap" between verses 1 and 2 of Genesis 1, during which time God created and then destroyed a "pre-Adamic race," is another speculation that is nowhere taught in the Scriptures.
- Certain groups handle deadly snakes and drink poison as part of their worship times in "obedience" to Mark 16:18!
- The identity of the Antichrist.
- The meaning of the "baptism for the dead" in 1 Corinthians 15:29.

This is where things can get dangerous. It becomes a very serious problem when speculations are presented as possessing the same degree of authority as "Level 1" direct statements of Scripture. Due to a lack of theological training, many church leaders and Christians do not have a balanced view of the degrees of doctrinal authority, but they have a "flat" theology in which everything they believe is considered to possess the same absolute authority. In such churches, aberrant speculations are believed and held to as zealously as direct statements of Scriptures, and sometimes even more so.

Strangely, in some churches, "Level 5" speculations are stated and pursued as pure and absolute revelations from God, whereas foundational "Level 1" doctrines are disregarded as unimportant ("that's just 'doctrine,' and 'doctrine' is not so important!"). Of course, the opposite is the truth: foundational doctrines are important, speculations are not.

Obviously, you should not give your life for someone's speculation. Unfortunately, however, in small, "cultic" churches, many believers have done just that.

We need to know the Word of God, and we need to know it in a balanced manner:

As I urged you when I went into Macedonia, stay there in Ephesus so that you may command certain men not to teach false doctrines any longer nor to devote themselves to myths and endless genealogies. These promote controversies rather than God's work – which is by faith. (1 Tim. 1:3-4)

In essence, Paul says to avoid speculation and focus on sound doctrine that is solidly based on the Scriptures. Stop worrying about peripheral issues and get into the Word – into matters that count, matters that will build you up and help you fulfill God's purpose.

He must hold firmly to the trustworthy message as it has been taught, so that he can encourage others by sound doctrine and refute those who oppose it. For there are many rebellious people, mere talkers and deceivers, especially those of the circumcision group. They must be silenced, because they are ruining whole households by teaching things they ought not to teach – and that for the sake of dishonest gain. (Tit. 1:9-11)

Dear friends, although I was very eager to write to you about the salvation we share, I felt I had to write and urge you to contend for the faith that was once for all entrusted to the saints. (Jude 3)

Jude says to contend for "the faith." He is speaking of foundational doctrine. We should not contend for someone's theory, however attractive it may seem.

For us to discern and fulfill the purpose of God for our lives, we need to know the Word, and to know the Word in a balanced way. We need to know the difference between a direct authoritative statement of Scripture on the one end of the scale, and a speculation from human reasoning on the other end. We need to rightly divide the Word of Truth (2 Tim. 2:15).

People waste years and sometimes their whole lives, never coming close to their purpose in God, because they get caught up in their own or someone else's religious speculations. This frequently happens in churches.

Furthermore, when a believer has a "flat" theology and he embraces all doctrines as "Level 1" for which he should die, then he will be in trouble when someone points out the error of one of his (in reality Level 5) beliefs. This will frequently happen because Level 5 doctrines do not have scriptural integrity and can be disproved easily. Since everything he believes forms the bedrock foundation of his Christian life – instead of only the top level beliefs forming his foundation – he will suffer a spiritual crisis and will not know what to believe anymore. His entire belief system will unravel. On the other hand, a believer who has a clear understanding of the different levels of authority of what he believes will be able to examine, adjust and occasionally reject, his lower level beliefs, while safely holding to the doctrines that matter the most.

Consider Paul's words in Philippians 3, after he has taught about the deep things of God:

> *All of us who are mature should take such a view of things. And if on some point you think differently, that too God will make clear to you. Only let us live up to what we have already attained. (Phil. 3:15-16)*

Clearly, Christians in any church are at various degrees of maturity and understanding. There are many different levels of teaching they have received and experiences they have had. Some will not understand the deep things Paul has just taught in previous verses. Significantly, Paul does not speak "down" to them, but as a friend. They may disagree with him, and if they do, Paul trusts God to help them see the Truth. Significantly, this refers to the deeper things of God; on the core issues of the faith, Paul does not allow such flexibility (e.g., Rom. 16:17-18; Gal. 1:8-9)!

Concerning the many *minor* issues about which Christians differ, you should:

1. Learn to distinguish between major issues and minor ones (Matt. 23:23). Build your life on the major issues.

2. Learn to distinguish between matters of command and matters of freedom (Rom. 14:14, 20).

3. On debatable issues, cultivate your own convictions (Rom. 14:5).[4]

4. Allow your brother the freedom to determine his own convictions – even when they differ from yours (Rom. 14:1-2).

5. Let your liberty be limited, when necessary, by love (Rom. 14:13 – 15:2).

6. Follow Christ as the Model and Motivator of servanthood (Rom. 15:1-3).

7. Pursue unity among the brethren (Rom. 15:5-7). This appeal for unity is a direct statement of Scripture!

Knowing God Himself is more important than splitting hairs about fine points of peripheral issues. Nevertheless, there is no contradiction between knowing God and knowing His Word.

You Must Know the Word of God

Your attention to the Word of God will probably determine whether you find and fulfill God's purpose for your life. Consequently, if you are seeking the true purpose of God in your life, then you will take the Word off the bookshelf, dust it off and get into it, and get it into you.

Many Christians ask others what they think God wants them to do, when they should instead spend their time in God's Word. That is where the answers are! Instead of asking someone else for their opinion, or trying to get a prophetic word from someone, get into the Word. It will help you. The more you know the Word of God, the more you will understand His will for your life.

---

[4] In Philippians 3, Paul shows us the balance: live according to your own conscience (v. 16) but give your brother the freedom to grow in his convictions (v. 15).

You need to diligently study the Word. Moreover, you need to do it as a habit, as a discipline; not just when the mood strikes you or the wind blows you. Some people will tell you that God hasn't "led" them to study the Bible recently. Yet, it seems that He apparently did lead them to get up every morning and go to work, to eat and to sleep! Of course God doesn't need to "lead" someone to do those things; and neither does He need to "lead" you to study His Word! You should be in the Word of God every day, whether you feel "led" or not.

Spending time in the Word of God should be one of the normal habits of your life. But remember: the only habits you develop are the habits that you develop!

To put it another way: you will start getting into the Word when you start getting into the Word. It is that simple. When you deliberately set yourself to be diligent and consistent in the Word of God, you will become spiritually strong.

Your Bible is not going to suddenly come before you and open itself before your eyes and speak to you and say, "Read me." You need to do it. The only habits you develop are the habits that you develop!

Furthermore, if you have time for breakfast, then you have time for the Word of God. If you have time for sports, then you have time for the Word of God. If you have time to start a business, then you have time for the Word of God. The Word of God is your life. You need the Word of God for life, for strength, and for direction in your life.

The Word will help you understand your purpose. The Word of God will help you make sense of your life. It will help you understand your past. It will help you plan for the future. It will help you to know and do God's will and purpose.

Misuses of the Word of God

Many Christians who would never have anything to do with the occult, nevertheless seek divine guidance in ways that are either directly or dangerously close to divination.

Some believers play "Bible roulette" to seek God's direction for their lives. They let their fingers walk through the Bible's pages, seeking some kind of guidance as they scan the words. If a verse pops out at them while they're scanning, they believe that is what God is saying to them.

Others let their Bible flop open at a particular passage or verse and accept that as the voice of God. There's a well-known fable of the man who was trying to find God's will for his life. He shut his eyes, opened up his Bible at random, and put his finger on a passage. Opening his eyes, he read the passage from Matthew 27:5, "Then he went away and hanged himself." Feeling the need for better direction than this, he closed his eyes again and opened his Bible to another passage. He looked and read Jesus' statement in Luke 10:37, "Go and do likewise." That wasn't quite what he was looking for either, so he tried one more time. He shut his eyes, opened his Bible, and read Jesus' words in John 13:27, "What you are about to do, do quickly"!

Other believers misuse the biblical account of Gideon's fleece in Judges 6:36-40. When trying to determine God's will, they "put out a fleece." Usually, however, the fleeces they put out require nothing like the super-natural intervention that Gideon's fleece required. Gideon's fleece was not merely a circumstantial sign. If your fleece does not require intervention that is absolutely supernatural – not just unlikely, or abnormal, but absolutely impossible except for a bona-fide supernatural intervention from God – then you have not followed the biblical example. In other words, if you are going to lay out a fleece, then lay out a good one! Gideon asked for two miracles from God. His odds were not 80 to 20 or even 99 to 1. What Gideon asked for was utterly impossible. He asked for two miracles, and he received them both. If you will lay out fleeces that are of truly biblical proportions, you may find that they are not answered anywhere near as often!

Moreover, although God gave Gideon the miracles he asked for, that does not mean He approved of such a method of determining His will. The use of fleeces is not repeated elsewhere in the Scriptures.

How the Word of God Helps Us Know God's Will

The answers for many of the questions of your life and purpose will be in God's Word in either one of two ways: specifically or in principle.

1. Specifically.

The issue you are interested in may be directly addressed in the Bible and God's will clearly revealed. For example, sexual immorality is specifically dealt with many times in the Bible:

It is God's will that you should be sanctified: that you should avoid sexual immorality; that each of you should learn to control his own body in a way that is holy and honorable, not in passionate lust like the heathen, who do not know God; (1 Thess. 4:3-5)

There is no doubt about whether or not fornication is permissible for a Christian!

Likewise, there are many specific questions that are easily answered by the Word. For example, does God want a Christian to marry an unbeliever? Many women have married an unbelieving man, thinking and hoping that God would change his heart, or that they would change his heart, after marriage. It rarely happens. The Word would have answered this question for them and spared them much grief (1 Cor. 7:39; 2 Cor. 6:14-15). You don't need someone to prophesy over you about issues like this since God has already told you what to do.

Does God want a Christian doctor to perform abortions? Does God want a Christian businessman to take on a new account if he would have to bend the rules of ethical conduct just a little to keep that account? The answers to these and many other questions are plainly revealed in the Bible. Consider the following Scriptures, all of which clearly address specific situations in our lives:

> *...But if you suffer for doing good and you endure it, this is commendable before God. To this you were called, because Christ suffered for you, leaving you an example, that you should follow in his steps. (1 Pet. 2:20-21)*

> *Wives...be submissive to your husbands... (1 Pet. 3:1)*

> *Husbands, love your wives, just as Christ loved the church and gave himself up for her (Eph. 5:25)*

> *Do not repay evil with evil or insult with insult, but with blessing... (1 Pet. 3:9)*

All these passages, and hundreds of others like them, give us clear biblical direction for specific situations in our lives. As the following table[5] demonstrates, God has laid out very clear revelations of His will concerning even our inner attitudes.

---

[5] Adapted from Garry Friesen & J. Robin Maxson, *Decision Making and the Will of God* (Sisters, OR: Multnomah Publishers, Inc., 1980), 156.

God's Will for Our Attitudes		
Is...	Is Not...	Key Passages
Love	Lust	Mark 12:28-31; Rom. 14:13-19; 1 Cor. 13:1-3; Rom. 13:14
Reliance	Independence	Prov. 3:5-6; Gal. 5:16
Humility	Pride	Jam. 4:6; Phil. 2:5-8
Gratitude	Presumption	Col. 3:17
Clear Conscience	Guilt	Rom. 14:22-23
Integrity	Irresponsibility	Col. 3:17, 22
Diligence	Laziness	Col. 3:23
Eagerness	Compulsion	1 Pet. 5:2
Generosity	Selfishness	1 Tim. 6:17-19
Submission	Self-advancement	1 Pet. 5:5-6
Courage	Cowardice	John 16:33; Matt. 10:26-28
Contentment	Greed	Heb. 13:5; Phil. 4:11

The Bible gives us extensive guidance on everything from A to Z, a fact graphically illustrated by Psalm 119 which contains 22 sections beginning with the 22 letters of the Hebrew alphabet. These sections show us the place of the Word of God in the Christian's life.

> *Oh, how I love your law! I meditate on it all day long. Your commands make me wiser than my enemies, for they are ever with me. I have more insight than all my teachers, for I meditate on your statutes. I have more understanding than the elders, for I obey your precepts. I have kept my feet from every evil path so that I might obey your word. I have not departed from your laws, for you yourself have taught me. How sweet are your words to my taste, sweeter than honey to my mouth! I gain understanding from your precepts; therefore I hate every wrong path. (Ps. 119:97-104)*

God gave us His Word to reveal His will for us. The Bible is so comprehensive that many times people who are trying to excuse their sin will claim that the issue is not mentioned specifically in the Bible. For example, someone may ask, "Where does the Bible say you can't take recreational drugs?" However, neither does the Bible say you shouldn't jump out of an airplane without a parachute. Look it up in your concordance and you will see that such a commandment is nowhere found – in any of the translations!

Thus, while there are many specific questions we can find answered, there are also clear principles in the Word that will help you discern God's will and purpose for your life concerning issues that aren't specifically addressed.

2. In principle.

Dr. Erich Klinger at the University of Minnesota conducted a study and found that each of us face between 300 and 17,000 decisions every day! Certainly, the exact answers to each of these questions are not all found in the Bible.

Since the Scriptures do not directly address many issues that we face, in prayer we should take the principles that are taught in the whole counsel of God and apply them to our specific situation. In this regard, there are certain passages that apply very well to a whole range of questions.

For example, Paul's statement in 1 Corinthians 6:19-20 would keep a Christian from taking recreational drugs (including nicotine), even though their use is not specifically prohibited in the Bible:

> Do you not know that your body is a temple of the Holy Spirit, who is in you, whom you have received from God? You are not your own; you were bought at a price. Therefore honor God with your body. (1 Cor. 6:19-20)

Moreover, we should dress in a manner that glorifies God in

our bodies. That also is applying this Scripture in a practical manner in our lives.

Thus, there are many Scriptures that we can apply to our lives, even though they don't directly address our specific questions. There are also broad principles taught in the Bible which can be applied to a large range of situations. For example:

> *So whether you eat or drink or whatever you do, do it all for the glory of God. (1 Cor. 10:31)*

> *And whatever you do, whether in word or deed, do it all in the name of the Lord Jesus, giving thanks to God the Father through him. (Col. 3:17)*

Take these principles, bathe them in prayer, and you will many times have a clear understanding of what God's will is concerning many issues that are not otherwise dealt with in the Scriptures.

This is one reason why you must study the Word of God. If you were given a book that had your name written on the front, and the title of that book was, "God's will for Bill," and the will of God for you was clearly set out inside, would you read that book? You would devour it!

Of course, the Scriptures do not read like a grocery list for your life. They aren't quite that clear. There are at least three reasons why they aren't:

1. The Scriptures are written for many other people, places, times and cultures as well as you.

2. With increased revelation comes increased responsibility. This means that if His will were crystal clear on every issue and you did not do it, your judgment would be stricter.

3. God does not want merely to tell you what to do; He also wants to deal with your heart and life along the way. Consequently, it is a journey, a journey of discovery.

Although the Bible is not written as a grocery list or a road map, if you will study it and learn it, as the Holy Spirit helps you and illuminates His Word to you, then you will have a much clearer knowledge of His purpose for your life.

Chapter 6

You Discern God's Purpose Through the Thoughts of Your Mind

The second way to know God's will is through the illumination of the Holy Spirit on the thoughts of your mind.

> *It seemed fitting for me as well, having investigated everything carefully from the beginning, to write it out for you in consecutive order, most excellent Theophilus, (Luke 1:3, NASB)*

Luke investigated, researched, studied and thought, and then he wrote, by the inspiration of the Holy Spirit, the infallible and inerrant Word of God. This is very significant!

God gave you a mind, and He gave it to you to use. American culture is very feeling-oriented. We are an experience-oriented society. This has crept into the church to the point that, in some circles, believers don't think very highly of their minds.

Many Christians would prefer a good feeling over a good thought any day of the week! Nevertheless, God gave you a mind, and He commanded you to love Him with all of it (Matt. 22:37)! It was not the devil who gave you a mind. In fact, it is just as easy for the devil to manipulate your feelings as it is for him to manipulate your mind – probably easier.

God commands us to use our minds to discern His will.

> *Examine yourselves to see whether you are in the faith; test yourselves.... (2 Cor. 13:5)*

> *Be diligent to present yourself approved to God, a worker who does not need to be ashamed, rightly dividing the word of truth. (2 Tim. 2:15)*

It would be considerably less work to merely have a dream or have a feeling, and know God's perfect will for your life all the time, but it doesn't work that way. God wants you to think.

Many times in his letters, Paul uses logic. He doesn't say, "Well, such and such is so, because I had a vision and that's that." Instead, he leads the believer through a process of rational thought. He does this many times. Jesus did this as well – over and over again (cf. Acts 2:25-31).

In giving us His Word, God did not say, "I'm God, here's the truth, now believe it." He could have said that. If He had said that, we would have no choice but to believe Him since He's God.

There are times in our lives when we have no other choice than simply to believe God, whether or not we understand. However, many times God also leads us through the process of investigating, discovering and understanding truth, and understanding His purpose for us. He wants us to understand with our minds. Naturally, we should not do this apart from Him, but our minds must be illuminated by His Spirit.

God does not want us to limit Him by the limitations of our minds; but, as much as possible, He wants our minds to be involved in the Christian life.

> *... be transformed by the renewing of your mind... (Rom. 12:2)*

According to Romans 12:2, your mind has a central part to play in your overall life transformation.

So, use your mind to discern God's will:

- Study His Word.
- Study your life.
- Ask Him for His help to make proper sense of it all.

Furthermore, there is nothing wrong with some plain old common sense. In fact, a little bit of common sense goes a long way in spiritual matters. Many of the cults and unhealthy church groups that people get involved with usually require the suspension of rational thought and common sense.

On the subject of common sense, consider the following humorous example of the dispute between Jim Dunn and the First Congregational Church of Akron, Ohio:

> It seems that Mr. Dunn believed that God told him to go live outside First Congregational. So he took his dog and set up housekeeping in a tent in the front yard of the church. At the time the article appeared from the Associated Press in *The Baton Rouge Morning Advocate*, Mr. Dunn, dog and tent had been in place there for some thirteen months. Mr. Dunn could have used a shelter two blocks from the church, but that was not where God had told him to go. Apparently, he also received some sort of revelation about taking showers – he abstained from such. He refused a new sleeping bag to replace the soiled one he had been using and rejected gifts of food unless the donor specified that it had come in response to God. "I'm not living my will," Mr. Dunn allowed, "I'm living God's will…"

> For all that, we prefer Mr. Dunn's clarity of purpose to the muddleheaded idiocy of the Reverend Bob Mollard, the administrative minister for the church, who is reported to have said, "If God called Jim to live in our front yard, who are we to say God didn't."

Well, Mr. Mollard may have difficulty in saying that God did not call Jim Dunn to live in the front yard of the First Congregational Church of Akron, but we have no difficulty at all in saying it. Nor do we have any difficulty in saying that neither did God call anyone as theologically ignorant and incompetent as Mr. Mollard to the ministry.[6]

God gave you your mind for you to use in serving Him. Your mind is not necessarily unspiritual. You should not limit God to what your mind can comprehend, and your mind does need to be renewed by the Word and Spirit; but, in itself, the mind is not unspiritual.

> *My message and my preaching were not with wise and persuasive words, but with a demonstration of the Spirit's power, so that your faith might not rest on men's wisdom, but on God's power. We do, however, speak a message of wisdom among the mature, but not the wisdom of this age or of the rulers of this age, who are coming to nothing. No, we speak of God's secret wisdom, a wisdom that has been hidden and that God destined for our glory before time began. (1 Cor. 2:4-7)*

> *We have not received the spirit of the world but the Spirit who is from God, that we may understand what God has freely given us. This is what we speak, not in words taught us by human wisdom but in words taught by the Spirit, expressing spiritual truths in spiritual words. The man without the Spirit does not accept the things that come from the Spirit of God, for they are foolishness to him, and he cannot understand them, because they are spiritually discerned. The spiritual man makes judgments about all things, but he himself is not subject to any man's judgment: "For who has known the mind of the Lord that he may instruct him?" But we have the mind of Christ. (1 Cor. 2:12-16)*

In these verses, Paul does not condemn the mind itself; he condemns the carnal mind. He does not condemn wisdom; he condemns limiting God to mere human wisdom.

---

[6] *The Concerned Presbyterian* (Vol. 1, Issue 2), Summer quarter, 1996; p. 12.

The carnal mind does not properly understand the things of God; they are foolishness to him. But the renewed mind (the mind of Christ) does understand the things of God.

As we grow in God and experience greater union and communion with Jesus, the more we will possess the mind of Christ as our minds are renewed by His Word and Spirit and as we are transformed into Jesus' image. The more our minds are transformed, the more we will understand the things of God, the more our minds will be able to grasp eternal realities, and the more our minds will be useful tools to help us know God's purpose.

There are two things we must understand regarding the mind:

1. On the positive side, God gave you your mind, not the devil. God wants you to love Him and serve Him with your mind. As you grow in Christ, your mind will be transformed into His image, and become more and more spiritually wise and useful to you.

2. Nevertheless, we must also acknowledge the inherent finiteness of our minds. Our minds have limitations. Our minds will not ultimately be able to grasp everything in God. Consequently, we should not trust in our own understanding (Prov. 3:5). Moreover, there is always the need for faith, for trust in God in spite of uncertainty and unclearness.

Antinomies

There will be many tensions in our Christian lives. As we seek to serve God and fulfill His purpose, these tensions will occur repeatedly.

An "antinomy" is a contradiction, a conflict of authority, a paradox. "Anti" means against; "nomos" means law. There are many antinomies in the Christian life.

Sometimes the antinomies are only apparent. Sometimes they are actual. These are contradictions that will probably never be resolved for us. They are ultimate paradoxes.

For example, the triune nature of God is impossible for our minds to grasp. The Father is God. The Son is God. The Holy Spirit is God. All of God is in the Father. All of God is in the Son. All of God is in the Holy Spirit. They are distinct but not separate. There is one God. God is one divine Spirit who eternally manifests Himself as the Father, Son and Holy Spirit. This is impossible for our minds to resolve. How can God be three and one at the same time?

Consider also, the creation of the world out of nothing.

> *By faith we understand that the universe was formed at God's command, so that what is seen was not made out of what was visible. (Heb. 11:3)*

How could God make something out of nothing? Your mind cannot understand that. You are not capable of understanding that. However, you can believe it.

These are ultimate antinomies. They will probably never be resolved to our full understanding in this life.

There will always be things that finite beings simply cannot comprehend, such as the nature of God and the creation of all things out of nothing. But that is not bad. It's not bad that you can't understand that; you're not supposed to understand it. So accept it; embrace it. Embrace those contradictions. Embrace those paradoxes.

Another antinomy is the relationship between the sovereignty of God and the genuine responsibility of man.

On the one hand, the Scriptures clearly teach that God is sovereign:

...the Most High is sovereign over the kingdoms of men and gives them to anyone he wishes."...All the peoples of the earth are regarded as nothing. He does as he pleases with the powers of heaven and the peoples of the earth. No one can hold back his hand or say to him: "What have you done?" (Dan. 4:32-35)

In him we were also chosen, having been predestined according to the plan of him who works out everything in conformity with the purpose of his will, (Eph. 1:11)

But who are you, O man, to talk back to God? Shall what is formed say to him who formed it, "Why did you make me like this?" Does not the potter have the right to make out of the same lump of clay some pottery for noble purposes and some for common use? (Rom. 9:20-21)

On the other hand, the Scriptures also teach that man is genuinely responsible:

...God...commands all people everywhere to repent. (Acts 17:30)

for, "Everyone who calls on the name of the Lord will be saved." (Rom. 10:13)

Again, this is an ultimate antinomy. This issue will probably never be resolved to our full understanding. Nevertheless, you should accept this paradox.

We get into trouble when we don't accept the antinomies that the Bible presents and we try to resolve them in a manner that makes sense to us. Then we get into trouble.

Consequently, some Calvinists end up with a God who is so sovereign that man is no longer genuinely responsible, and it doesn't matter what anyone does. Thus, there is no need for evangelism. Their attitude is: "If God wants to save the lost, He'll save them without our help."

On the other hand, some Arminians make God's will subject to the will of man. They teach that God looked down through history and saw what men would choose to do and then He foreordained that. Consequently, the will of man becomes the final sovereign purpose in the universe and God is no longer truly sovereign. Unfortunately, if God is no longer truly sovereign, then God is no longer truly God!

There are many ultimate contradictions in God that will never be resolved. Our minds need to accept the reality that there are issues that are beyond our mental comprehension. That fact in itself should be intellectually satisfying to us. There are things in God that we, as created beings, simply cannot grasp. Since we are created beings, it is both logical and intellectually satisfying that we cannot fully comprehend our Creator and His plan.

Moreover, these antinomies are not only theological. Our daily lives are filled with apparent antinomies as well.

We encounter apparent antinomies when we go through things we don't understand, but later realize what actually happened. We can see what God was doing; we can understand it now. But at the time it didn't make sense. At the time it appeared to be a contradiction. At the time we couldn't understand it.

Can you imagine the disciples standing at the foot of the cross looking up at the Man whom they had followed for three years, the Man who came to be King – yet now, here He was, hanging as a despised, rejected criminal, dying on a cross? What a devastation to them! What a contradiction. How could they understand that? How could they reconcile what Jesus had said to them about Himself – about His deity and His Kingship – with what was happening to Him now? They couldn't, could they?

However, three days later, they could! After the resurrection, it all made sense.

Many times in our lives, God will allow things to happen that are paradoxes. At times He will allow terrible things, painful things, contradictory things, things that make no sense at all at the time. It is only later that they will make sense.

We must trust God anyway. We should try to understand His ways and His purposes in everything, but we must not limit God to what we can understand. We must accept the contradictions. We must embrace the contradictions. We must trust God even when we can't figure it out.

This will prevent you from becoming offended at God when He does things differently from how you would have done them, or how you thought He would do them. God knows what He's doing; and He does have purpose. You may not be able to perceive it at the time, but hold on to God and it will all make sense in the end.

> *And we know that in all things God works for the good of those who love him, who have been called according to his purpose. (Rom. 8:28)*

In the end, it will all work out for your good and for His glory.

Job went through extraordinary sufferings. In the end of the story, however, Job was blessed and, most importantly, God was glorified.

> *As you know, we consider blessed those who have persevered. You have heard of Job's perseverance and have seen what the Lord finally brought about. The Lord is full of compassion and mercy. (Jam. 5:11)*

You will be blessed in the end; so endure now. Endure, in spite of the contradictions.

The reality of Christian suffering can be a stumbling block to many in the "Faith camps" around the world. There have been many teachers who stress a very aggressive faith in God and in His promises, but not all of them leave room in their theology for God to be God. As a result, many Christians have been offended when things didn't turn out as promised. They stumbled when it didn't work. They stumbled because they had not embraced the whole counsel of God.

For example, the Bible does teach divine healing and that God will provide for us physically and financially as well as spiritually. But the same Bible that teaches a message of faith also teaches, with equal force, a message of suffering: a message of apparent defeat many times. The same Bible that teaches you to boldly go before the throne of God and claim His promises also teaches you that God remains sovereign, not you and not your faith. God is in charge. He determines, ultimately, what happens.

We should be aggressive in our faith, but our understanding of God has to be big enough so that we still follow Him even when it does not work – even when the bottom falls out of your life.

One of the greatest statements of faith in the Bible was made by the three Hebrew boys to King Nebuchadnezzar:

> *If we are thrown into the blazing furnace, the God we serve is able to save us from it, and he will rescue us from your hand, O king. But even if he does not, we want you to know, O king, that we will not serve your gods or worship the image of gold you have set up. (Dan. 3:17-18)*

They had a strong faith in God ("the God we serve is able to save us… and He will rescue us from your hand"), yet they submitted themselves to God's sovereign will at the same time ("but even if He does not…").

The Bible contains many examples of men and women who walked with God and believed His promises for them, and yet things did not always go the way they would have liked. It was not always peaches and cream for them!

Joseph, for example, faced severe contradictions. His circumstances did not make sense. He was supposed to be blessed by God and yet his life was one disaster after another. Finally, he lay in prison:

He sent a man before them, Joseph, who was sold as a slave. They hurt his feet with fetters, He was laid in irons. Until the time that his word came to pass, The word of the Lord tested him. (Ps. 105:17-19, NKJV)

The word of God tried him. The promises of God to Joseph tested him. Joseph was tried and tested. It did not make sense. His circumstances were a complete contradiction to the promises God had given him. Yet in the end he understood it:

You intended to harm me, but God intended it for good to accomplish what is now being done, the saving of many lives. (Gen. 50:20)

...it was to save lives that God sent me ahead of you...God sent me ahead of you to preserve for you a remnant on earth and to save your lives by a great deliverance. So then, it was not you who sent me here, but God... (Gen. 45:5-8)

Similarly, there are many great saints mentioned in Hebrews 11:

Some faced jeers and flogging, while still others were chained and put in prison. They were stoned; they were sawed in two; they were put to death by the sword. They went about in sheepskins and goatskins, destitute, persecuted and mistreated – the world was not worthy of them. They wandered in deserts and mountains, and in caves and holes in the ground. These were all commended for their faith, yet none of them received what had been promised. (Heb. 11:36-39)

These were men and women of strong faith. You don't need faith when everything is going well. Real faith is continuing to trust God even when it doesn't work – even when it doesn't make sense – knowing that He is faithful and that in the end it will work out and He will be glorified.

How the Holy Spirit Illuminates Your Mind

There are a number of ways that God will reveal His will to you through your understanding:

1. Specific interest.

As much as you would like to, you cannot do everything. Consequently, God will lay specific situations, needs or areas of ministry upon your heart. For example, He may give you a strong sense of compassion for an individual. The world may be filled with many great needs, but the Holy Spirit focuses your mind upon this particular person. In this way, God is speaking to you, revealing His specific direction for you.

2. Priorities.

We all face priority decisions about the many commitments we are asked to make. By His Spirit, God will give us understanding about what our priorities must be. He will help us to distinguish what is important in specific situations in the light of His eternal values.

3. Spiritual wisdom.

Perhaps in the majority of situations we will not have a specific, direct word from God about what His will for us is. Nevertheless, we can still proceed with confidence when we make decisions according to the spiritual wisdom He progressively gives us. This is one of the primary ways in which we discern God's will through the Holy Spirit's illumination of our understanding. This is spoken of many times in the Scriptures:

God gave Solomon wisdom and very great insight, and a breadth of understanding as measureless as the sand on the seashore. (1 Kings 4:29)

Reflect on what I am saying, for the Lord will give you insight into all this. (2 Tim. 2:7)

As for you, the anointing you received from him remains in you, and you do not need anyone to teach you. But as his anointing teaches you about all things and as that anointing is real, not counterfeit – just as it has taught you, remain in him. (1 John 2:27)

And this is my prayer: that your love may abound more and more in knowledge and depth of insight, so that you may be able to discern what is best and may be pure and blameless until the day of Christ, (Phil. 1:9-10)

For by the grace given me I say to every one of you: Do not think of yourself more highly than you ought, but rather think of yourself with sober judgment, in accordance with the measure of faith God has given you. (Rom. 12:3)

We all need wise insight to lead our lives in a manner that will bring God glory and fulfill His purposes. Fathers need wisdom to lead their families (1 Pet. 3:7; Eph. 6:1-2). Church leaders need wisdom to lead God's people (Acts 6:3). Employers need wisdom to treat their workers properly (Col. 4:1).

As we submit to God, apply ourselves to His Word, and seek Him for wisdom, He will give it to us:

If any of you lacks wisdom, he should ask God, who gives generously to all without finding fault, and it will be given to him. (Jam. 1:5)

This will not always mean quick and easy answers. In fact, God rarely reveals His will for us as a road-map or grocery list of instructions.

As one biblical scholar said, "Wisdom is the endowment of heart and mind needed for righteous conduct of life."

We acquire wisdom through:

- Asking God for wisdom.
- The various gifts God has given us.
- The Word of God.
- The experiences of our lives.
- Personal learning and research.
- Wise counselors and mentors.
- The Holy Spirit who puts all of the above together and builds it into spiritual wisdom.

When we mature in wisdom before God, we will be able to make correct decisions for our lives without a divine grocery list or road-map. This is one of God's primary ways of leading us: through the spiritual wisdom He works in us. Thus, in many of the matters of life we are able to make wise decisions, without waiting on a vision or audible voice from God, fully confident that we are moving in a direction consistent with His purpose.

Chapter 7

You Discern God's Purpose Through the Inner Witness in Your Heart by His Spirit

One day I walked into a factory. I was in the presence of God and the Lord spoke inwardly to me by His Spirit, "Today is Hector's day." Hector was an Hispanic man I knew at this factory. Emboldened by this inner witness, I spoke aggressively to Hector about the Lord Jesus and his need for salvation. That day Hector received Jesus as His Lord and Savior, and was filled with the Holy Spirit! Several months later, Hector was killed in an accident. By God's grace, he was saved in time!

There are many Scriptures that specifically speak about this inner witness of the Holy Spirit.

> *But when the time had fully come, God sent his Son, born of a woman, born under law, to redeem those under law, that we might receive the full rights of sons. Because you are sons, God sent the Spirit of his Son into our hearts, the Spirit who calls out, "Abba, Father." (Gal. 4:4-6)*

According to these verses, the Holy Spirit is in our hearts and He "calls out." The Holy Spirit in our hearts says things; He speaks. His is not simply an unfelt and theoretical presence that we accept by faith: but the Holy Spirit does things and says things.

Those who obey his commands live in him, and he in them. And this is how we know that he lives in us: We know it by the Spirit he gave us. (1 John 3:24)

It is not an intellectual knowledge referred to here, but an inward spiritual perception. It is an experience. It is not just a mental realization that since we're keeping His commandments therefore He must abide in us whether we inwardly perceive it or not. The point of this verse is that if you keep His commandments, then you abide in Him and He abides in you; and you know He abides in you by the inner presence of the Spirit in your heart. That's how you know He's there. You inwardly perceive His presence. You inwardly experience His fellowship.

This has several important implications. As you obey God, you abide in Him and He abides in you, and you experience that abiding. It is an actual, inward spiritual experience. Therefore, as you obey God more, you will experience Him more! You will grow in your inward fellowship with Him more. You will grow in your ability to perceive His inward voice, His inward witness. This is how you grow in your ability to hear the inward voice of the Holy Spirit: you obey God.

We know that we live in him and he in us, because he has given us of his Spirit. (1 John 4:13)

It is not just "by faith" that we have God's presence – it is also an experience.

Anyone who believes in the Son of God has this testimony in his heart... (1 John 5:10)

Here the word "testimony" is used. This word is also translated "witness" in other translations. In our hearts, we have the witness, or testimony, of the Spirit.

But the Counselor, the Holy Spirit, whom the Father will send in my name, will teach you all things and will remind you of everything I have said to you. (John 14:26)

According to John 14:26, the Holy Spirit in us will speak to us.

But when he, the Spirit of truth, comes, he will guide you into all truth. He will not speak on his own; he will speak only what he hears, and he will tell you what is yet to come. He will bring glory to me by taking from what is mine and making it known to you. All that belongs to the Father is mine. That is why I said the Spirit will take from what is mine and make it known to you. (John 16:13-15)

These verses do not just refer to prophetic ministry, although they obviously include that. But they refer primarily to our inward relationship with God by His Spirit. The Holy Spirit in us speaks to us. He reveals Jesus to us. The Holy Spirit reminds of what Jesus said. Oftentimes, the inward witness of the Spirit will be a quickening of the Word of God to our particular situation, bringing to our remembrance what Jesus said.

The Holy Spirit in us glorifies Jesus. He lifts Jesus in our inward consciousness and thereby glorifies Him.

because those who are led by the Spirit of God are sons of God. (Rom. 8:14)

The Spirit himself testifies with our spirit that we are God's children. (Rom. 8:16)

These two verses in Romans 8 are best understood when taken in their context. In Romans 7, Paul deals with man's struggle with sin. Then in Romans 8, he sets forth our victory in Christ: our victory is a daily life of walking with God, obeying God. Thus, the context is obedience to God; not a legalistic outward adherence to a set of rules, but an inward submission to God, obeying Him from our heart, walking in fellowship with Him, living life by His indwelling life. Paul's context is the believer walking daily in the Spirit, overcoming sin by His life, growing in the personal knowledge of the Lord Jesus. That is the context in which verses 14 and 16 are written.

Again the implication is powerful: if you want to hear the voice of God in a greater way, if you want to discern His purpose for your life and for particular situations, then walk with Him, die to self, surrender to Him, obey Him, love Him, fellowship with Him. That's how it works. As we grow in Christ and as we mature in His Word, we grow in our ability to hear His voice inside our hearts.

> *Whoever has my commands and obeys them, he is the one who loves me. He who loves me will be loved by my Father, and I too will love him and show myself to him...If anyone loves me, he will obey my teaching. My Father will love him, and we will come to him and make our home with him. (John 14:21-23)*

In John 14, Jesus said that He and the Father will manifest themselves to us as we obey His Word.

This idea of the inner witness of the Spirit is bigger than us simply living our lives and doing what we want, and then asking God to give us the answer to some problem we're facing, hoping that we can hear His voice.

The context of the inner witness of the Spirit is a life of fellowship with God: a daily life of offering up ourselves to God, of fellowship with God, of growing in God, of being transformed by His Word and His Spirit, of being conformed to His image.

Sin Hinders the Inner Witness of the Spirit

Since the way we grow in our capacity to hear God's voice inwardly is to obey Him, the biggest hindrance to knowing this inward witness from God is sin.

Many Scriptures reveal the hardness of the heart that comes through sin:

> *But encourage one another daily, as long as it is called Today, so that none of you may be hardened by sin's deceitfulness. (Heb. 3:13)*

Sin hardens your heart against God. In Ephesians 4, Paul describes those who are lost:

> *They are darkened in their understanding and separated from the life of God because of the ignorance that is in them due to the hardening of their hearts. Having lost all sensitivity, they have given themselves over to sensuality so as to indulge in every kind of impurity, with a continual lust for more. (Eph. 4:18-19)*

The progression in this verse is that sin produces hardness of heart, which produces ignorance of God and separation from His life.

If left unchecked, sin and its corresponding hardness of heart will result in the believer falling away.

> *The Spirit clearly says that in later times some will abandon the faith and follow deceiving spirits and things taught by demons. Such teachings come through hypocritical liars, whose consciences have been seared as with a hot iron. (1 Tim. 4:1-2)*

Thus, the chief enemy of the inward witness of the Spirit is sin.

The Characteristics of the Inner Witness of the Spirit

Some characteristics of the inner witness of the Spirit are:

1. This is not an inwardly audible voice necessarily. It is a "witness," an inward certainty, an inner sense or perception. That is the New Testament terminology: the witness of the Holy Spirit

inside our hearts. Sometimes it will be an inwardly audible voice, but usually it is a more subtle witness.

2. This witness is not an emotional feeling.[7] Although the two are very often confused, the inner witness of the Spirit is deeper than that.

If people make an error concerning discerning this inner witness, they usually mistake their emotions for it. That is the most common error.

Many times in giving personal prophecies, people mistake their own positive feelings for someone as a direction from God and pronounce a prophetic word of blessing to the person, when, in reality, it's not a word from God at all. This happens many times.

> *After David was settled in his palace, he said to Nathan the prophet, "Here I am, living in a palace of cedar, while the ark of the covenant of the Lord is under a tent." Nathan replied to David, "Whatever you have in mind, do it, for God is with you." That night the word of God came to Nathan, saying: "Go and tell my servant David, 'This is what the Lord says: You are not the one to build me a house to dwell in.'" (1 Chron. 17:1-4)*

> *...Say to those who prophesy out of their own imagination: "Hear the word of the Lord!" (Ezek. 13:2)*

> *This is what the Lord Almighty says: "Do not listen to what the prophets are prophesying to you; they fill you with false hopes. They speak visions from their own minds, not from the mouth of the Lord." (Jer. 23:16)*

---

[7] We can have an emotional or intellectual *response* to the inner witness of the Holy Spirit, but that response is not the Spirit's witness itself.

I did not send these prophets, yet they have run with their message; I did not speak to them, yet they have prophesied. (Jer. 23:21)

Today, this is usually the product of immaturity and not the intention to deceive. Thus, the solution to this problem is to grow in God.

The opposite can also happen. God may actually be leading you in a certain direction, but you mistake His inward leading for your own "feelings" or for your own thoughts.

My wife had a repeated inner impression to check the freezer in the garage. She dismissed this as her own thoughts. When eventually she did go into the garage, she discovered the freezer lid had been left open by our young son. All along, God had been leading her to check it! This often happens in our lives. When we are not sensitive enough to God's inner leading, we miss many opportunities.

Thus, the confusion of our own thoughts or emotions for God's witness goes both ways.

3. The inner witness of the Spirit can be either positive ("I have a peace about it") or negative ("I have a check in my spirit. I don't feel right about this.").

    The more you grow in God, the more sensitive you will become to this inner leading, and the more you'll learn to distinguish it from your emotions and from your own thoughts.

4. The inner witness of the Spirit must line up with the Word of God.

    If your inward witness disagrees with the clear teaching of the Word of God, you must reject it. Always, without exception, the Word of God must be given first place in your life, or you will end up in serious error and deception.

Ideally, all six ways of discerning God's purpose should agree. The Word and our own thoughts and the witness of the Spirit, and the counsel of others, and so forth, should all agree.

However, they may not always agree. Sometimes in my life, my thoughts were to go in one direction, but then the witness of the Spirit in my heart led me in another direction. Then, as things proceeded, it became obvious what the Lord's plan really was, and, at that point, my thoughts lined up. For example, many years ago, I decided that God wanted me to plant a church in Russia and to live there for the first couple of years, raising up local leadership. But, over a short period of time, the Holy Spirit gently showed me that I was wrong. Consequently, another brother led the church and I did not, and that was indeed the purpose of God.

Your thoughts do need to line up with the Holy Spirit's leading sooner or later, and if it is God, then they will.

However, the clear teaching of the Word of God should never contradict your thoughts or your inward witness. If that is the case, you need to stop and find out what the problem is. Either you do not understand the Scriptures correctly or you're not in tune with the right voice inwardly.

I once knew a man who divided a local church on the basis of his revelation about a particular idea. When I confronted him with the fact that his revelation was unscriptural, his response was to say, "The Holy Spirit who is in me, who is my teacher, will not allow me to accept your interpretation." In reality, this man had a vested interest in not accepting my interpretation, even though my interpretation was plainly correct.

I learned something from that experience: a person who will not submit to the clear teaching of the Word of God usually has some vested interest in another direction that they're trying to justify through their own "inward leading from the Holy Spirit."

I have seen a number of people over the years follow their own inward impressions in spite of the clear Word of God, and end up destroying their own lives and the lives of others around them. The Holy Spirit, however, will never lead someone in a direction that contradicts the teaching of the Word of God.

In Ephesians 4, Paul describes spiritual maturity in the following way:

> *Then we will no longer be infants, tossed back and forth by the waves, and blown here and there by every wind of teaching and by the cunning and craftiness of men in their deceitful scheming. (Eph. 4:14)*

5. The inner witness of the Holy Spirit is based upon surrender to God.

    This brings us back to our first point: the only basis upon which you will successfully know and fulfill God's will for your life is first to surrender to Him. It is only as you surrender to God that you will learn to know His voice inwardly through the inner witness.

6. You will grow and mature in this ability to discern the inner witness of the Spirit.

    You will mature:

    - as you grow in God,
    - as you learn His Word and your mind is renewed,

- as you overcome temptations on a daily basis,
- as you resist sin and its hardening of your heart,
- as you endure the sufferings and tribulations He allows you to experience, without being offended with God or man,
- as you grow in your prayer life,
- as you allow God to break your pride, self-will and stubbornness.

As you mature in God, then your ability to hear His inward voice will become clearer and clearer.

It will also help if you read some books on this subject. For example, *The Practice of the Presence of God* by Brother Lawrence, or *Experiencing the Depths of Jesus Christ through Prayer* by Jeanne Guyon.

There is no substitute for spiritual maturity. Furthermore, there are no crash-courses in spiritual maturity. It is a growth.

This is a paradox. On one hand, the newest believer who has received Christ and the indwelling Holy Spirit, can and should hear God's inward voice. On the other hand, it takes time, faithfulness and pain to consistently know the inward voice of God.

Chapter 8

You Discern God's Purpose Through Prophetic Revelation from God

We can discern God's will through prophetic revelation from God. This prophetic revelation can include dreams, visions, angelic visitations, the audible voice of God, and the revelatory gifts of the Holy Spirit.

We need prophetic revelation. We do not need this to establish new doctrine or to give us new books for the Bible. However, we do need prophetic revelation to help us wrestle with discerning God's purpose, to encourage us and strengthen us, to confirm clear direction and occasionally to expose our hearts and things in our lives that we have either missed or are deliberately ignoring.

> *During the night Paul had a vision of a man of Macedonia standing and begging him, "Come over to Macedonia and help us." After Paul had seen the vision, we got ready at once to leave for Macedonia, concluding that God had called us to preach the gospel to them. (Acts 16:9-10)*

I received a prophetic word from a brother one day. We had just had lunch together and were talking and he said, "I feel impressed to say this to you...." It was a simple thing for him, but it was quite meaningful to me, and it encouraged me concerning some particular issues I was dealing with.

In our church one Sunday morning, a sister shared a word of knowledge that God wanted to heal one person of a neck problem received in an accident, and another person of athlete's foot. She said it was God's desire to reveal His love to them in that way. Later that day, I discovered a couple had visited our church that morning. They had been recently delivered from a cult, and were struggling in their newly-found Christian lives. They had just asked God to reveal Himself to them in a greater way and to confirm that they were on the right track spiritually. She had been in a car accident and had the neck condition. He had the athlete's foot. They were both healed that morning during the worship!

The New Testament church is a prophetic church.

> *In the last days, God says, I will pour out my Spirit on all people. Your sons and daughters will prophesy, your young men will see visions, your old men will dream dreams. Even on my servants, both men and women, I will pour out my Spirit in those days, and they will prophesy. (Acts 2:17-18)*

The church of Jesus Christ is a prophetic people. Prophetic revelation should be the norm and not the exception in our lives.

Prophetic ministry in the church has not passed away:

> *It was he who gave some to be apostles, some to be prophets, some to be evangelists, and some to be pastors and teachers, to prepare God's people for works of service, so that the body of Christ may be built up until we all reach unity in the faith and in the knowledge of the Son of God and become mature, attaining to the whole measure of the fullness of Christ. (Eph. 4:11-13)*

God's intention is that prophetic ministry be present in His church until the church has come to full maturity. That has not happened yet, so prophetic ministry is still in the church.

Therefore you do not lack any spiritual gift as you eagerly wait for our Lord Jesus Christ to be revealed. He will keep you strong to the end, so that you will be blameless on the day of our Lord Jesus Christ. (1 Cor. 1:7-8)

Paul, in 1 Corinthians 1, also states that all the gifts of the Holy Spirit are to be in the church until the time of the coming of the Lord Jesus. The gifts of the Holy Spirit have never passed away.

According to Jesus, the Holy Spirit will show us things to come. This is one aspect of the normal everyday ministry of the Holy Spirit in the life of the normal everyday believer.

But when he, the Spirit of truth, comes, he will guide you into all truth. He will not speak on his own; he will speak only what he hears, and he will tell you what is yet to come. (John 16:13)

Prophetic revelation should be the norm in the lives of men, women, young people and children:

In the last days, God says, I will pour out my Spirit on all people. Your sons and daughters will prophesy, your young men will see visions, your old men will dream dreams. Even on my servants, both men and women, I will pour out my Spirit in those days, and they will prophesy. (Acts 2:17-18)

Prophetic ministry is not just for the leaders of the church. Throughout the church, the prophetic should be the norm, because the Holy Spirit is in us all, and, as we have seen, He speaks to us and through us.

God wants all the saints to walk in the realm of the supernatural and in the realm of the prophetic to some degree.

For you can all prophesy in turn so that everyone may be instructed and encouraged. (1 Cor. 14:31)

We are a prophetic people. The prophetic should be the norm in the church of Jesus Christ.

Levels of Prophetic Authority

All prophetic ministry is not the same. It does not all carry the same degree of authority. Just as there are levels of doctrinal authority, so there are varying levels of prophetic authority. As the objectivity of the revelation increases, the authority of the revelation increases.

1.   Prophetic impressions.

The beginning levels of prophetic revelation include inward prophetic "impressions." These are genuine revelations from God and can be very specific and accurate. However, they can also be affected by our own feelings and ideas. They are more subjective than other "higher" forms of revelation.

2.   Special illumination.

This is when the conscious sense of the Lord's presence, or the anointing of the Holy Spirit, gives special illumination to our minds. This will give us greater confidence that we are hearing from God, but these revelations can still be influenced significantly by our own thoughts and feelings. Examples of this kind of revelation would be clear inward words of knowledge or wisdom, or clear dreams.

3.   Open visions.

Open visions occur on a higher level than inward impressions. These are external visions. It may be, for example, that the wall you are looking at disappears and you are viewing, as it were, a movie screen, on which God gives you a specific and clear vision. This kind of revelation can also include hearing the audible, external voice of God (e.g., 1 Sam. 3:4). Because these revelations are external, there is less possibility of mixture. They are more objective and thus more authoritative since they involve less possibility of human error or involvement.

4. Trances.

There are several biblical instances of trances (e.g., Acts 10:10ff; 22:17ff). In a trance, instead of viewing a "movie screen," you are actually involved in what is happening around you. You are there. Trances can range in intensity from mild trances, in which you are still conscious of your physical surroundings, to trances in which you feel like you are literally in the place of your vision. This is probably what Ezekiel experienced in his revelations, and also what John experienced when he had the visions of the book of Revelation.

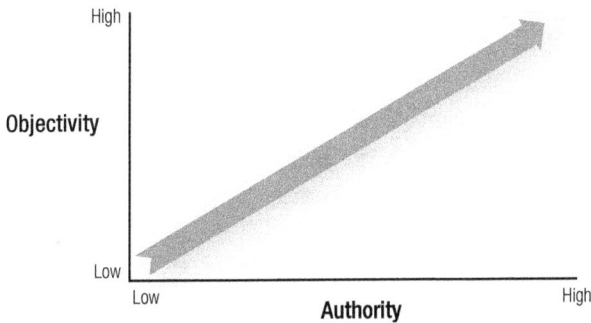

Higher forms of prophetic revelation carry a higher level of authority, since they are more objective. Revelations that are less objective and more subjective carry less authority. There is a direct relationship between the level of objectivity of a revelation and the authority it carries.

That does not mean that since you only had an impression and someone else had a trance or an open vision, therefore your impression is wrong. It does not mean that impressions are not of God. However, you must recognize that there are varying levels of prophetic authority, and so don't "bet the farm" on someone's impression!

Your inward impression may well be from God, but don't demand that someone sell their house, quit their job and move to Africa, just because you had an impression that they are called to minister there.

Many people have done this. They have received a personal prophecy, based upon someone's inward impression, and obeyed it, only to later discover it was not God. There are many men who were told they would be great evangelists. Some of these men lived for years under condemnation because they were not winning the lost as they thought they were supposed to. However, God had never, in reality, called or gifted them to do this.

Moreover, we should not be embarrassed about asking people what kind of revelation they had. If someone says to you, "God said thus and so," ask them, "How did God say thus and so? Did you hear an audible voice or see an external vision, or was it an inward impression?" This will not intimidate someone who is truly gifted prophetically and secure in God.

Since the New Testament church is prophetic, and since we do have an abundance of prophetic revelation coming forth in this day, we need to be wise in how we interpret and apply revelation, or else we will likely find ourselves running hither and yon following someone else's subjective impressions.

We must also recognize that there is a great mixture of prophetic voices out there. Consequently, we must test the prophetic word. God tells us to do this.

Interpreting and Applying Prophetic Ministry

There are three parts to prophetic ministry that must be kept distinct:

1. The revelation itself. What is the revelation?
2. The interpretation of that revelation. What does it mean?
3. The application of that interpretation. What do we do about it?

For example, in Genesis 41, Pharaoh had two dreams (revelation) that no one, including himself, could understand. Then Joseph gave Pharaoh the meaning of the dreams (interpretation), and also told him what to do (application).

Just because someone has a genuine revelation does not necessarily mean they have the correct interpretation or application of that revelation. Therefore, there is the need for the whole body to function in prophetic ministry. There is also the necessity of wise pastoral oversight of this ministry.

Encouraging Prophetic Ministry

Leaders can set the tone for prophetic ministry in meetings:

1. By teaching the people on the gifts of the Spirit.
2. By asking God to reveal His Son in supernatural ways.
3. By consistently encouraging people to expect the revelatory gifts.
4. By building a sense of excitement about hearing from God.
5. By affirming that when we cry out to God in faith, He will come and speak to us.
6. By gently encouraging at appropriate times. For example, during a quiet moment in worship ask, "Is the Lord speaking to anyone's heart right now?"

In encouraging prophetic ministry, certain safeguards should be observed:

1. Don't be over-awed by revelatory gifting. It's not good for the church or for the person if you take everything they share as "direct from God." Dare to challenge and question (in a kind way) and keep things light.
2. Gently enforce the standard of "positive encouragement only" when allowing this type of ministry. Never let prophetic ministry become an exposé of a person's supposed shortcomings or sins.

3. Prophecy that is directive ("Go to India and be a missionary"), corrective ("God is correcting you about this or that") or negative ("I had a dream in which you died in a car accident") should not be given without first seeking counsel from an appropriate authority figure in the local church.

4. From the beginning, keep accountability high. When a specific word is given, ask the person being ministered to, "Does this witness to you?" Give permission by the tone of the meeting for him to say "No," if need be. This can set up a healthy learning environment for all present – if there is no blame or shame allowed at the same time.

5. Do not constantly look to one highly gifted person. If you have one of these in the church, help them learn to mentor and equip others in this ministry. If everyone understands that prophetic gifting is no more glamorous than any other, some will be saved from the "spiritual star" mentality and many struggles with pride later on.

6. Do not be intimidated by a person gifted in this way, especially if you feel you have no strength in this area personally. The leader has a leadership anointing and the spiritual responsibility to take the oversight in the church. No matter how "gifted" an individual may be, they have no right to overrule God's authority in the local church.

7. The purpose of the revelatory gifts is not to establish doctrine. The author cringes whenever he reads of some famous "prophet" who says, "I was wondering about a certain doctrine and so I said to God, 'What does this mean?' and here's what He said to me..." God gave us His Word to establish doctrine. It may be more work to study and learn, but it is much safer!

Testing Prophetic Ministry

God tells us to test the prophetic word. We need to not only know how to test prophetic words, but we need to be comfortable doing so without feeling threatened or intimidated.

"From my perspective, the single greatest failure in my own traditional Pentecostal movement, a failure I find repeated over and over again in the second and third waves of this movement, is that of letting almost anything go for fear of quenching the Spirit." (Gordon Fee)

That is a sobering statement from a great Pentecostal scholar! So we need to understand what the Bible says about testing the prophetic.

There are several clear injunctions in the Bible to test prophetic ministry:

> *Let two or three prophets speak, and let the others judge. (1 Cor. 14:29, NKJV)*

The rest of the church ("the others") are supposed to judge the words of the prophets.

> *Dear friends, do not believe every spirit, but test the spirits to see whether they are from God, because many false prophets have gone out into the world. (1 John 4:1)*

It is not "unspiritual" to test prophetic ministry. It is not rebellion against God. In fact, it is rebellion against God to not test prophetic ministry because He commands us to do this!

We should not feel under pressure to mindlessly embrace every prophetic word we ever hear. God tells us to test it.

> *Do not quench the Spirit, do not despise prophesying, but test everything; hold fast what is good, abstain from every form of evil. (1 Thess. 5:19-22, RSV)*

First Thessalonians 5:19-22 should not have been translated as four separate paragraphs as in the King James Version, but as a single paragraph, because it is really one progressive thought.

In this passage, Paul gives an excellent balance. He gives the balance between not quenching prophetic ministry, on the one hand, and yet not allowing just anything to go on in the name of the prophetic, on the other. Notice also that the first thing he says is not to quench the Spirit. His priority here is that we do have prophetic ministry. Paul's priority is not so much to stamp out the wrong but to encourage the right.

Furthermore, the word that is translated "test" means "to test with the expectation of approving." It is not a negative, critical testing that is in view here. Paul is not referring to testing and expecting to reject it all. In essence, he instructs us to test because we know God has given us prophetic ministry, and we gratefully receive that ministry as valid, and we want that ministry to be functioning at peak performance. That is what our mindset should be.

It is interesting that Paul does not tell us how to test prophetic ministry in 1 Thessalonians 5. He simply says to do it. He does not give us a list of ways to tell a right prophecy from a wrong one. He simply says, "Test it, and hold fast to the good, and forget the wrong."

Probably the reason he does not give a list of tests here is because the Scripture elsewhere has already given us much on this subject. There are many scriptural ways to test prophetic ministry.

1.   The test of consistency with the Word of God.

> But even if we or an angel from heaven should preach a gospel other than the one we preached to you, let him be eternally condemned! (Gal. 1:8)

Are these words or directions balanced doctrinally? How do they check out against the revelation of the Scripture?

> Concerning the coming of our Lord Jesus Christ and our being gathered to him, we ask you, brothers, not to become easily unsettled or alarmed by some prophecy, report or letter supposed

to have come from us, saying that the day of the Lord has already come. Don't let anyone deceive you in any way, for that day will not come until the rebellion occurs and the man of lawlessness is revealed, the man doomed to destruction...

So then, brothers, stand firm and hold to the teachings we passed on to you, whether by word of mouth or by letter. (2 Thess. 2:1-3 with v. 15)

2.   Does it come to pass?

If what a prophet proclaims in the name of the Lord does not take place or come true, that is a message the Lord has not spoken. That prophet has spoken presumptuously. Do not be afraid of him. (Deut. 18:22)

But the prophet who prophesies peace will be recognized as one truly sent by the Lord only if his prediction comes true. (Jer. 28:9)

This rather obvious test of prophetic ministry is neglected frequently. It is sad to see people rushing, year after year, to listen to the same "prophets" whose previous prophecies did not come to pass. For example, many popular ministries predicted great disaster involving the Y2K bug. Moreover, every year the same ministries predict international financial collapse and ruin. Ultimately, God will judge the world, but in the meantime His cause is not assisted by overzealous and immature ministries.

Of course, sometimes God will give conditional prophecies. For example, Jonah's prediction of Nineveh's destruction (Jonah 3:4) was not fulfilled because Nineveh repented.

3. Does it lead people to God?

> *If a prophet, or one who foretells by dreams, appears among you and announces to you a miraculous sign or wonder, and if the sign or wonder of which he has spoken takes place, and he says, "Let us follow other gods" (gods you have not known) "and let us worship them," you must not listen to the words of that prophet or dreamer. The Lord your God is testing you to find out whether you love him with all your heart and with all your soul. (Deut. 13:1-3)*

Does the prophetic word or ministry cause people to be led towards the worship of the true God, or do they get sidetracked in another direction?

Does the prophetic ministry exalt Jesus, and lead people to a greater surrender and commitment to Him, or does it exalt a man and lead people to a greater devotion to some church or human ministry?

We're not suggesting that God would never affirm or confirm a particular local church or ministry. Nevertheless, an awful lot of "prophetic back-scratching" does go on today.

True prophetic ministry, however, will exalt the Lord Jesus, and not man and his programs.

4. The test of fruit.

> *Watch out for false prophets. They come to you in sheep's clothing, but inwardly they are ferocious wolves. By their fruit you will recognize them. Do people pick grapes from thornbushes, or figs from thistles? (Matt. 7:15-16)*

Outward success of a ministry is not a guaranteed test of its authenticity. We have all seen many ministries which once looked so successful, yet they fell by the wayside when hidden sin was revealed.

It is not outward success we're looking for, but whether or not the one sharing the "prophetic" word has integrity and character. I have met many "prophets" over the years whose personal lives and families were a mess and yet they fully expected to be taken seriously as delivering the oracles of God! They demanded to be taken seriously, and got very upset when it was pointed out that their lives did not line up with their so-called gifting.

Character does matter. In fact, it is the main issue. If you want to be taken seriously in any ministry – prophetic or otherwise – work on your character, and then your gift will make a way for itself. This does not mean you have to be perfect, but you do need integrity and character. Moreover, people with prophetic ministries must submit themselves and their ministries to the oversight of the local church's leadership; they must live and minister in genuine accountability.

5.   Does it build up or tear down?

> *It was he who gave some to be apostles, some to be prophets, some to be evangelists, and some to be pastors and teachers, to prepare God's people for works of service, so that the body of Christ may be built up until we all reach unity in the faith and in the knowledge of the Son of God and become mature, attaining to the whole measure of the fullness of Christ. (Eph. 4:11-13)*

According to Ephesians 4, the purpose of the prophet is to build up the body of Christ, to help transform the body into the mature image of Jesus Christ. This is confirmed by 1 Corinthians 14 that also states that the specific purpose of the gift of the prophecy is to build up:

> *But everyone who prophesies speaks to men for their strengthening, encouragement and comfort. He who speaks in a tongue edifies himself, but he who prophesies edifies the church. I would like every one of you to speak in tongues, but I would rather have you prophesy. He who prophesies is greater than one who*

speaks in tongues, unless he interprets, so that the church may be edified. (1 Cor. 14:3-5)

This does not mean that God would never have a negative word for His people; but, even then, the clear intention and purpose, as well as the result of the prophetic word will always be to build up and strengthen, not to attack, beat down and destroy.

The previous test (4) is the fruit of their lives; this test (5) is the fruit of their ministries.

6. The test of confirmation.

Generally, the word should confirm an existing direction and not set the precedent. This is why people should be encouraged to speak further with someone who shares a prophetic revelation with them. Additionally, the recipient should be asked, "How does that word sound to you? Does it confirm what God has been telling you?"

The prophetic word should confirm what God has already been telling you. But, if it does not, then set it aside. God is not going to expel you from His Kingdom just because you don't receive a word from someone when that word is totally meaningless to you, or when it doesn't line up with what the Lord has already been showing you. So, set it aside; put it on the shelf.

If it lines up with the first five tests of prophetic revelation, it may be from God. However, don't be brought into bondage to it, if it doesn't confirm what God is already doing in your life. Leave it on the shelf. Then, perhaps go back to it once in a while and check it out. It may mean a lot to you in a year, even though it doesn't mean much now. But don't be brought into bondage to it.

God wants prophetic ministry to be a blessing to His body and not a curse!

Chapter 9

You Discern God's Purpose Through the Counsel of Others

Where there is no counsel, the people fall; But in the multitude of counselors there is safety. (Prov. 11:14, NKJV)

Listen to advice and accept instruction, and in the end you will be wise. (Prov. 19:20)

God can reveal His purpose to you through the spiritual wisdom of others.

In receiving counsel from others, there are two extremes to avoid:

- Receiving no counsel.
- Receiving too much counsel.

1.   No counsel.

I've known a number of people over the years who said, "I'm not going to look to man for counsel. The Lord is my Counselor! I'm going to get counsel from His word and from His word alone."

On the surface, that attitude sounds spiritual. However, if you would actually read the Word and obey it, you would discover that the

Word of God itself tells us that we need, at times, to receive counsel from people who God has placed in our lives to give us counsel.

Obviously, this needs to be godly counsel, rooted in the Word of God, and proceeding from a life that is surrendered to the Lord and experienced in His ways. Consequently, this can become not merely the counsel of man, but the very counsel of God. Thus, this can be a way that God reveals His will to you.

> *...fools despise wisdom and instruction. (Prov. 1:7, NKJV)*

> *Without counsel, plans go awry, But in the multitude of counselors they are established. (Prov. 15:22, NKJV)*

> *Plans are established by counsel; By wise counsel wage war. (Prov. 20:18)*

> *A wise man is strong, Yes, a man of knowledge increases strength; For by wise counsel you will wage your own war, And in a multitude of counselors there is safety. (Prov. 24:5-6)*

2.   Too much counsel.

The opposite extreme is just as bad. Some people seek counsel from anyone and everyone, instead of looking to God and His Word. They end up receiving much counsel that is worldly and bad. Confusion results from either having too much counsel or the wrong kind – or, too much of the wrong kind!

> *He who walks with the wise grows wise, but a companion of fools suffers harm. (Prov. 13:20)*

> *Blessed is the man who does not walk in the counsel of the wicked or stand in the way of sinners or sit in the seat of mockers. (Ps. 1:1)*

Thus, in receiving counsel, we need discernment and balance.

The Characteristics of Godly Counsel

1. **Godly counsel is based on the Word of God.**

    Blessed is the man who does not walk in the counsel of the wicked or stand in the way of sinners or sit in the seat of mockers. But his delight is in the law of the Lord, and on his law he meditates day and night. (Ps. 1:1-2)

    In getting counsel from others, we need to reject the wisdom of man and embrace the wisdom of God.

    and how from infancy you have known the holy Scriptures, which are able to make you wise for salvation through faith in Christ Jesus. All Scripture is God-breathed and is useful for teaching, rebuking, correcting and training in righteousness, so that the man of God may be thoroughly equipped for every good work. (2 Tim. 3:15-17)

    Sanctify them by the truth; your word is truth. (John 17:17)

2. **Godly counsel must deal with heart issues, and not just externals.**

    In both these aspects, the wisdom of the Bible differs greatly from the wisdom of modern man.

    For example, the following table contrasts certain aspects of modern wisdom with godly wisdom.

Modern Wisdom	Biblical Wisdom
The wisdom of the world is the guide for the problems of practical living. The Bible is a good "resource" for "spiritual issues" such as ethics or religious experience.	The Bible is the all-sufficient, relevant, comprehensive, final authority on all the practical issues of life, as well as so-called "spiritual" ones.
Our ultimate purpose lies in ourselves.	Our ultimate purpose lies in God.
Our goal is self-fulfillment.	Our goal is death to self and the glory of God.
We are the helpless victims of life and of others' wrongdoings.	We are responsible for our own choices and responses.
The means of change is for the "inner child" to be "healed," or to spend years in psychotherapy or some other humanistic method which encourages self-absorption.	We need to repent, forgive others, take responsibility for our lives and obey God.

According to modern wisdom, the Bible is fine to use for certain "spiritual" issues, but, when it comes to the practical issues of life, we should forget the Bible since it is irrelevant.

Years ago, when I worked in a nursing home, I wanted to bring some Bibles in. The lady in charge said, "What a wonderful idea! Old people like to hold the Bible when they feel lonely or depressed." That is how modern man views the Scriptures: as something "nice," but essentially irrelevant to the real issues of life.

However, the Bible represents itself as the all-sufficient, relevant, comprehensive, final authority on all the practical issues of life, as well as so-called spiritual ones. The Scripture gives us our guide for all life issues such as communication, conflict management, finances, child-rearing, our identity ("who am I?"), marriage, self-deception, motives, decision-making, deliverance from addictions, what to do when we are sinned against, how to be delivered from anger, anxiety, unforgiveness, and so forth.

Of course, the Bible doesn't always tell us what we want to hear. We prefer to hear that our ultimate purpose for existing lies in ourselves. We would rather believe that our ultimate goal in life is self-fulfillment, self-realization and self-actualization. We would rather believe that our goal is to do what we want to do, and to feel good.

The Bible, however, teaches that our ultimate purpose is to die to self, to do God's will and to glorify Him.

Moreover, we would rather believe that our lives are in a mess because of someone else's fault. We want to blame others for our condition. We would rather see ourselves as the poor, helpless, wounded victim.

However, the Bible makes us take responsibility for our own lives, for our own choices, for our own decisions, for our own responses to the bad things others may have done to us, and not to shift the blame to others when the consequences are not to our liking.

We are not responsible for the bad things others may have done to us, but we are entirely accountable to God for how we respond. We may have been greatly wronged by others in life, but that is not the actual cause of our problems. In reality, our problems are caused by how we responded to that wrong. So often, we respond to wrongs against us with bitterness, unforgiveness, self-pity and self-absorption. Consequently, we will only find release from the pain, and we will only find joy, peace and fulfillment, when we take responsibility for our own choices in life and embrace the purposes of God.

Thus, the means of change is not that some "inner child" needs to be healed, or that someone else needs to be punished for causing us suffering, but we need to repent and forgive, and get on with obeying God in our lives.

When we give counsel or advice to others, we need to be sure that what we say to others can be found in the Bible. We should not merely parrot the latest pop psychology craze to hit the church. We must discover the real issues of the heart and deal with them.

The Forms That Counsel Can Take

Godly counsel can take a number of different forms. Through counsel from others you may receive:

- confirmation (e.g., 1 Sam. 14:6-7; 23:17; 25:26-30; Esther 4:13-14; Luke 1:42-45; Acts 15:7-12),
- addition/guidance (e.g., Josh. 2:16; 17:14-18; Ruth 3:1-4; 1 Kings 1:11ff; 2 Kings 4:9-10; 5:2-3; Prov. 11:14; 12:15; 15:22; 19:20; 20:18),
- change/adjustment (e.g., 2 Sam. 20:16-22; 2 Chron. 29:3-12; Acts 5:35-39; Phil. 4:2), or
- correction (e.g., Ex. 18:14-24; 1 Sam. 25:26-31; 2 Kings 5:13; Ezra 10:10-11; Prov. 10:17; 12:1; 15:10; Jer. 26:15-19; Acts 19:30; Gal. 2:11).

Furthermore, godly counsel can be given in a variety of different ways:

1.   Public counsel.

This includes teachings, workshops, seminars, training events, small group meetings, etc.

Until I come, devote yourself to the public reading of Scripture, to preaching and to teaching. Do not neglect your gift, which was given you through a prophetic message when the body of elders laid their hands on you. Be diligent in these matters; give yourself wholly to them, so that everyone may see your progress. Watch your life and doctrine closely. Persevere in them, because if you do, you will save both yourself and your hearers. (1 Tim. 4:13-16)

Let the word of Christ dwell in you richly as you teach and admonish one another with all wisdom, and as you sing psalms, hymns and spiritual songs with gratitude in your hearts to God. (Col. 3:16)

Whatever you have learned or received or heard from me, or seen in me – put it into practice. And the God of peace will be with you. (Phil. 4:9)

2.   Self counsel.

Watch your life and doctrine closely. Persevere in them, because if you do, you will save both yourself and your hearers. (1 Tim. 4:16)

But his delight is in the law of the LORD, and on his law he meditates day and night. (Ps. 1:2)

3.   Sought counsel.

Then those who feared the LORD talked with each other, and the LORD listened and heard. A scroll of remembrance was written in his presence concerning those who feared the LORD and honored his name. (Mal. 3:16)

Brothers, if someone is caught in a sin, you who are spiritual should restore him gently. But watch yourself, or you also may be tempted. (Gal. 6:1)

See to it, brothers, that none of you has a sinful, unbelieving heart that turns away from the living God. But encourage one another daily, as long as it is called Today, so that none of you may be hardened by sin's deceitfulness. We have come to share in Christ if we hold firmly till the end the confidence we had at first. (Heb. 3:12-14)

4.   Unsought one-on-one counsel.

Do not hate your brother in your heart. Rebuke your neighbor frankly so you will not share in his guilt. (Lev. 19:17)

Let a righteous man strike me – it is a kindness; let him rebuke me – it is oil on my head. My head will not refuse it... (Ps. 141:5)

Better is open rebuke than hidden love. Wounds from a friend can be trusted, but an enemy multiplies kisses. (Prov. 27:5-6)

If your brother sins against you, go and show him his fault, just between the two of you. If he listens to you, you have won your brother over. (Matt. 18:15)

You hypocrite, first take the plank out of your own eye, and then you will see clearly to remove the speck from your brother's eye. (Matt. 7:5)

Brothers, if someone is caught in a sin, you who are spiritual should restore him gently... (Gal. 6:1)

My brothers, if one of you should wander from the truth and someone should bring him back, remember this: Whoever turns a sinner from the error of his way will save him from death and cover over a multitude of sins. (Jam. 5:19-20)

Fathers, do not exasperate your children; instead, bring them up in the training and instruction of the Lord. (Eph. 6:4)

5. **Unsought group counsel.**

> *But if he will not listen, take one or two others along, so that
> "every matter may be established by the testimony of two or three
> witnesses." If he refuses to listen to them, tell it to the church; and
> if he refuses to listen even to the church, treat him as you would
> a pagan or a tax collector. (Matt. 18:16-17)*

From Whom Should You
Receive Godly Counsel?

1. **Your parents.**

Even when you are old, you should still listen to your parents.

> *Listen to your father, who gave you life, and do not despise your
> mother when she is old. (Prov. 23:22)*

This does change somewhat as ones grows. After the woman
marries her first submission is no longer to her parents, but to
her husband (Eph. 5:22). Additionally, the husband is to "leave
his father and mother and be united to his wife" (Eph. 5:31).
Thus, one's primary allegiance is to one's spouse and not to
one's parents. But we should always respect, honor and listen
to our parents.

You should listen to your parents especially when you're young.

> *Children, obey your parents in the Lord, for this is right. "Honor
> your father and mother" – which is the first commandment with
> a promise – "that it may go well with you and that you may
> enjoy long life on the earth." (Eph. 6:1-3)*

2. Your spouse.

She speaks with wisdom, and faithful instruction is on her tongue. (Prov. 31:26)

Wives, submit to your husbands as to the Lord. (Eph. 5:22)

3. Church leaders.

Obey your leaders and submit to their authority. They keep watch over you as men who must give an account. Obey them so that their work will be a joy, not a burden, for that would be of no advantage to you. (Heb. 13:17)

4. Christian friends, spiritual mentors, spiritual fathers or mothers, etc.

He who walks with the wise grows wise, but a companion of fools suffers harm. (Prov. 13:20)

5. Other authority figures such as employers, school officials and government officials.

Submit yourselves for the Lord's sake to every authority instituted among men... (1 Pet. 2:13)

Naturally, the counsel we receive from unbelieving secular authorities will be limited to certain spheres of life.

God commands us to submit to those who are in authority over us, as long as they don't ask us to do something that would be clearly contrary to the will of God (e.g., Acts 5:29). Thus, when we submit to them, we're going to be relatively safe. When we rebel against authority figures, whether it be parents, spiritual authorities at church, secular authorities at work, or teachers at school, then we expose ourselves to danger.

God has given us many godly avenues for receiving counsel in our lives and we should avail ourselves of them, to help us to find His purposes for our lives.

Chapter 10

You Discern God's Purpose Through Understanding Your Life's Experiences

The final way of discerning God's purpose is by understanding our life experiences.

God sovereignly controls all things that happen:

> *In him we were also chosen, having been predestined according to the plan of him who works out everything in conformity with the purpose of his will, (Eph. 1:11)*

> *And we know that in all things God works for the good of those who love him, who have been called according to his purpose. (Rom. 8:28)*

Therefore, we can look at the circumstances of our lives – both past and present – to gain insight into His purpose.

We should not base our discernment of God's purpose solely upon the experiences of our lives, because it is easy to misinterpret outward circumstances (e.g., Acts 28:4-6).

Nevertheless, we need regularly to stop and meditate on our lives, asking God to give us insight into the experiences of our lives.

Too many people charge through life, never stopping to think what they should or should not be doing.

We need to stop and think, meditate, pray, and ask God for understanding. We need to think over our lives to understand them, because many times, where we've been will give us some excellent insight into where we should (or should not) be going.

Moreover, we should do this weekly, as part of our "Sabbath rests," concerning what we did that week.

Jesus told His disciples to rest (Mark 6:31). Leaders and busy disciples often do not do this. Sabbath rests do not make you more holy, but they will make you more healthy.

In our weekly Sabbath rests we should stop and look: backward, upward and forward.

- Backward: we should pause and reflect on the past week and consider its meaning and purpose.
- Upward: we should get before God and allow Him to reveal the motives of our hearts and bring alignment with His will and purpose. This should be a time of returning to eternal truths, sorting out the truths and commitments by which we are living, recalibrating our spirits, reaffirming what we believe and why we do what we do. This should be done through praying, reading, meditating and reflecting.
- Forward: We should look at what is coming in the future and meditate on its potential problems, opportunities and possibilities. Moreover, we should define our mission: looking to the future, affirming our intentions to pursue a Christ-centered tomorrow, pondering where we are headed in the coming days, defining our intentions and making our dedications.

We should also have periodic times of coming apart to seek God regarding the overall direction of our lives, and how it all fits together.

This is a very healthy thing to do for a few days each year, or more often.

In Acts 13:1-3, it seems that the leaders came together with no fixed agenda other than to worship God, and in that context the Holy Spirit gave significant new direction for Paul and Barnabas.

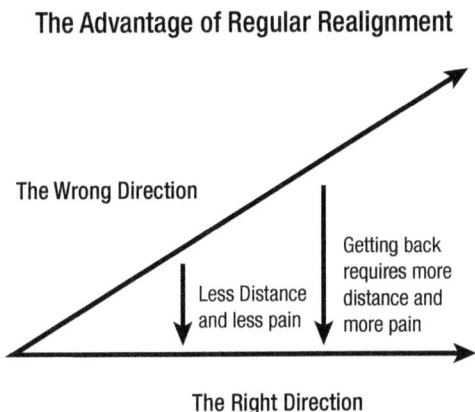

The Advantage of Regular Realignment

The Wrong Direction

Less Distance and less pain

Getting back requires more distance and more pain

The Right Direction

The more often we do this, the sooner we can bring our lives back on track if we are starting to miss our right direction. This will help us to build with gold, silver and precious stones instead of with wood, hay and straw (1 Cor. 3:12-15).

In this manner, we should align our lives frequently. What are our priorities? What are our values? How are we spending our time? Are we spending our time on the right goals, or is our time being wasted? How are we conducting our lives? Are we living in a Christian manner or are we living like the world?

One of the guiding Scriptures of my life is Colossians 4:17.

> *Tell Archippus: "See to it that you complete the work you have received in the Lord." (Col. 4:17)*

We all have a work to do, and God will one day hold us accountable for it. In order to fulfill His purpose, we must frequently align our lives. The more frequently we align our lives, the less painful it will be.

Understanding Your Experiences

You are a steward of the experiences God has given you in life. You are a steward of the maturity He has given you in many areas.

Our lives are like a work of needlepoint. When viewed from underneath, it is a confused mass of thread with no pattern or meaning. However, from the top, we can see the beauty of the intricate pattern – all the threads actually have meaning and purpose!

We need to examine our lives, seeking God's perspective of meaning.

Here are some questions that will help you clarify your lifelong quest for your specific purpose in life. These questions are keys to understanding what your life's purpose is. These are a few questions to ask that will help you as you meditate on the purpose of your life, to see what God has been doing in your life and what He's been preparing you for. These are questions to ask as you think back on your life, to significant experiences and relationships you have had.

As you go over each of these questions and slowly answer them, and as you meditate on your life, allow God to show you overall patterns and meaning in your life.

Write down some of what the Lord shows you at that time. Pray over it. You may gain some great insights into His purpose.

However, don't just do this once. Do it regularly. Also, you should add to these questions. These are just some ideas to get you started.

Deliberately Searching for God's Direction[8]

- Who are my models and mentors? Whom do I admire?
- Which biblical character(s) do I wish to be "like"? Why?
- Which biblical books, chapters or stories have affected me deeply? Why?
- Which books have really touched my life?
- What prophetic revelation have I received (from God directly, or others) regarding my gifts and calling?
- What do I think are my spiritual gifts? My natural talents?
- When have I grown the most as a person? As a leader?
- What are the key relationships God has given me?
- What kinds of needs are highlighted to my mind?
- What kinds of strategies does my mind easily and often develop?
- What have been my primary successes and fulfillments in life? What did I learn?
- When have I failed most painfully? What did I learn?
- In what context do I feel most motivated and zealous?
- In what context do I withdraw and resist? Why?
- Do I work best alone or in an interpersonal community?
- What kind of people do I enjoy the most? Why?
- What type of work setting or ministry environment do I appreciate most?
- What have others told me about my gifts and calling?
- What have others told me that I do well?
- What kind of assignments do others usually give me?
- Which habits, blind spots, or negative self-talk undercut my progress the most?
- What values, beliefs, or purposes do I hope to live out?
- If there were absolutely no limits on me, what would I choose to do?
- When have I known myself most candidly?
- What traumas have redirected me?
- Has an event stirred me so deeply that it caused me to vow to take action? What touches me?
- Whose love for me and belief in me has given me roots? Wings?

---

[8] Adapted from Robert D. Dale, *Leading Edge: Leadership Strategies from the New Testament* (Nashville: Abingdon Press, 1996), 44-45.

Your answers to the questions above and to others like them can supply you with some clues to your life's direction. Many of these clues are hidden within our histories and ourselves. Some clues are people; others are places and experiences. Sleuthing for your own life vision is one of the most exciting detective stories you'll ever "read" or write.

Furthermore, in meditating upon your life's experiences, the following are some valuable principles that will help you align your life with God's purposes for you.

1. **Your purpose may be found as you reflect on:**

   - Your head. What God has taught you. Your knowledge.
   - Your hands. What you have learned to do. Your skills.
   - Your feet. Where you have been. Your history.
   - Your heart. What you want to do. The passion God has placed in your heart.

   God is not wasteful. He intends to use your knowledge, skills, history and passion in His future purpose for you. Consequently, reflecting on these can help reveal His purpose.

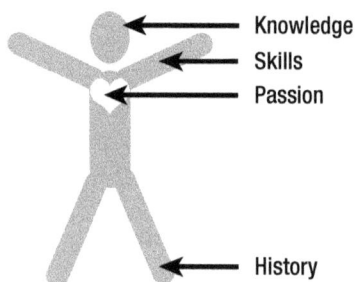

2. **Your purpose may be revealed by the divine connections given to you.**

   Your purpose is not found or accomplished in a vacuum, but in relationship with others. Thus, many times we can discern the purpose of God by considering the divine connections He gives us. He may put people around us whose gifts are the same as ours or complementary.

We have divine appointments in our lives all the time. God brings us into many relationships with other people, and this is not arbitrary; but it's part of His great overall plan.

Your life is filled with little "chance" meetings that you don't think much of at the time; yet, those connections can have profound significance down the road.

This is why you should meditate on the people God has brought you into contact with and on the purpose of that contact. With His help, understand those connections. Discover how they all fit together.

God brings you into relationship with others, so that you can affect their lives and so that they can affect yours. Moreover, this effect will be positive as well as negative. Some of the greatest learning and preparing experiences in your life have been through very negative situations – negative experiences and relationships that have molded you and that have given you the special abilities and wisdom you now have.

You are a steward of the relationships God gives you. Therefore, you need to think about your life, and allow God to show you how all the connections fit together, and how to best use for the future what He has already done for you.

3. Your purpose will be found and lived out in step-by-step obedience.

It is very unlikely that we will see it all at once and all in advance. But God leads us on step-by-step; and as we walk in obedience to what He's already shown us, He shows us more.

Many times God does not show us everything that is coming in the future because we would not be able to handle it. Other times He veils the future from us because if we knew what the future held, we would try to "make it happen."

> *The secret things belong to the Lord our God, but the things revealed belong to us and to our children forever, that we may follow all the words of this law. (Deut. 29:29)*

God opens the path of our life before us, step-by-step.

> *Therefore do not worry about tomorrow, for tomorrow will worry about itself. Each day has enough trouble of its own. (Matt. 6:34)*

4. God's purpose will be progressively revealed to you.

You may start out with a certain direction, and as you proceed along that path, a new path will open up to you. This new path could not have been seen from your initial starting point; but since you have moved, it is now revealed. Then as you head toward that goal, a further new goal will be revealed. This may be your final goal and purpose, but you would never have found it had you not moved along one step at a time pursuing your current understanding of His will.

For example, God did not reveal to Joshua the full extent of his ministry at one time. He revealed it to him gradually. Joshua was first Moses' assistant, then a warrior, then a leader, then he led

Israel into the possession of her inheritance, and finally he was the chief shepherd over the entire nation. Similarly, God's will for your life will be progressively revealed.

5. Faithfulness in little precedes responsibility for much.

As we show ourselves trustworthy with a little, God will progressively give us more:

> *Whoever can be trusted with very little can also be trusted with much, and whoever is dishonest with very little will also be dishonest with much. (Luke 16:10)*

This is a hard lesson for us, because we usually want to start at "the top."

We think God has called us to evangelize, and so we sit by the phone waiting for Reinhard Bonnke to call and invite us to preach to a half million Africans in one meeting. Meanwhile, our own neighbors are lost and dying, but we don't have time for them because we can't leave the phone. We're too busy trying to "hit the big-time"!

I know Christian ministers who are still waiting for the "big break" when God has called them to be faithful in a little, before He will give them more. They're waiting for the big break, and not being faithful in the little things He's given them responsibility for in the meantime. "The person who is too big for a small job, is too small for a big job."

If you consider the lives of men and women who ended up in world-wide, high-profile ministries that are effective and influential, you'll usually discover they had many years of blood, sweat and tears being faithful in little things prior to God opening the big doors. Even in the secular world, there are countless stories of people who spent many years becoming "overnight" successes.

Obey Him in a little and He'll give you more. Do something *little* with your life! It's a very healthy thing when you settle the simple fact that you are a nobody and get on with the job!

In any case, in the Kingdom of God, the reality is that nothing is little. As the saying goes, "The pay is the same in the end." Do what God has given you to do, whether it seems like a lot or a little, whether it seems important or insignificant. Do what He's given you to do, and you'll hear those wonderful words at the end, "Well done, thou good and faithful servant, enter thou into the joy of the Lord."

6.   Purposes grow and change.

As you obey God little by little and you walk step-by-step, His plan will begin to unfold before you. Although you may have understood it a certain way in the past, now you realize it is another way altogether.

This does not mean that His purposes change, but that your perception of His purposes grows and changes as you begin to see and understand more and more of it.

Therefore, don't tie yourself down to yesterday's vision, but let God mature and develop your vision the way He wants to. As you grow, change and mature, your vision will grow, change and mature. Stay supple and pliable. Allow God to mature you and to mature your vision.

7.   You must understand where your purpose fits in the corporate purpose of His church.

This is very difficult for Americans to do, because, fundamentally, we are very independent and individualistic. It comes naturally and easily for us to have a sense of individual purpose and destiny. It's much harder for us to see ourselves as parts of something bigger than us. It is hard for us to serve someone else's purpose; we want to serve our own.

However, an eternal principle is found in Luke 16:12.

And if you have not been faithful in what is another man's, who will give you what is your own? (Luke 16:12, NKJV)

In the Kingdom of God, to fulfill your purpose always requires you to help others fulfill their purposes. This is always the way it is in God. Consequently, if you're self-centered and self-absorbed, you will never understand or fulfill your purpose. But if you lift your eyes off yourself and serve others, working to help others fulfill their purposes, then you will fulfill your own purpose as well.

We must realize that we are only little fishes in a big lake, and that lake primarily is the local church where God has set us. This is why our own individual purposes and vision need to relate to the purpose and vision of the local church where God has set us.

Our individual purposes may be different, but they should still be aligned with the overall purpose of the church we're a part of. As each of us has an individual calling and gifting of God upon our lives for various purposes, those purposes have to serve the larger corporate purpose of the church where God has set us. We all should be working together to build the local body of Christ.

Some people think that God has called them to something "beyond the local church." Perhaps He has. However:

- As you head out to your broader scope of ministry the New Testament pattern is that, if that does actually happen, you will be sent out from, and remain accountable to, the local church where God has set you.
- If you've not first been faithful in your ministry in the local church, the broader ministry will not open up.

If God truly has called you to a broader ministry of some kind, then the proving and preparing ground for that ministry will be your local church.

I've met many people over the years who believed God had called them to something "big," and yet they never came into it. A likely reason for that is that they were waiting for some "ministry" to open up, and they were not faithful where God had set them. It was somehow "beneath them."

Before you can address multitudes somewhere else you must serve God in the little things where you are living now. Concentrate on doing that. Put the broader ministry on hold for a while and focus on little things, and you will be surprised at how well you do. The frustration will go and you will find fulfillment in serving God as you faithfully serve your brothers and sisters right where you are. He will open up new dimensions of your purpose in His time.

This is all part of the principle of serving others.

> And if you have not been faithful in what is another man's, who will give you what is your own? (Luke 16:12, NKJV)

If you will serve others, and help others to fulfill their purposes, you will be fulfilled.

If you are discontented with where you are now, if you feel like you've missed your purpose, then look back on your life and ask yourself, honestly, "Have I been serving others? Or am I still waiting for something great to open up for me?"

Serve others. Help others fulfill their purposes. If you'll do that, it will work out a whole lot better and you won't be frustrated.

When we're self-absorbed and self-centered, then we get frustrated and discontented.

So, don't be absorbed with the idea of some high and lofty purpose you think you have. Serve tables. Find a need and meet it. Get involved in serving, then God will open doors for you.

You should not do it with the mindset of "this is how I'll be released." That's like "giving to get." But serve others because you love them and because you love God. Do it sincerely and God will lead you into the fulfillment of His purpose for your life.

Chapter 11

Summary

In summary, according to the two principles of purpose, your purpose is found:

1. In the will of God.
2. In the pursuit of God.

The six specific paths to the discernment of God's purpose, through the illumination of the Holy Spirit, are summed up in the following table.[9]

These six will work together to give you an overall conviction regarding God's will.

You should consider all six when seeking to understand God's purpose for your life. Moreover, it is best to have all six in agreement when making a major decision.

That is a good model to follow!

---

[9] Adapted from Garry Friesen & J. Robin Maxson, *Decision Making and the Will of God* (Sisters, OR: Multnomah Publishers, Inc., 1980), 230.

Six Paths to the Discernment of God's Purpose, Through the Illumination of the Holy Spirit				
	Sphere:	Nature:	Means:	Governing Principle:
Word of God	Moral and spiritual decisions	Direct guidance	God's revealed commands and principles	The Word of God
Thoughts of Your Mind	Nonmoral decisions	Indirect guidance	Acquired wisdom	Spiritual wisdom
Inner Witness	Nonmoral decisions	Direct, but subjective, guidance	The abiding Holy Spirit	Holy Spirit's leading
Wise Counsel	Major decisions	Indirect guidance	The wisdom of others	Wise counsel
Prophetic Revelation	Special cases	Supernatural guidance	Visions, dreams, angelic visitations and prophecy	Prophetic revelation
Understanding Your Life's Experiences	In all things	Indirect guidance	God's sovereign control over all events	God's sovereignty

Selected Bibliography

Dale, Robert D. *Leading Edge: Leadership Strategies from the New Testament*. Nashville, TN: Abingdon Press. 1996.

Erickson, Millard J. *Christian Theology*. Grand Rapids, MI: Baker Book House. 1985.

Friesen, Garry and J. Robin Maxson. *Decision Making and the Will of God*. Sisters, OR: Multnomah Publishers, Inc., 1980.

Joyner, Rick. *The Final Quest*. New Kensington, PA: Whitaker House. 1996.

MacDonald, Gordon. *Ordering Your Private World*. Nashville, TN: Thomas Nelson Publishers. 1985.

Petty, James C. *Step By Step: Divine Guidance for Ordinary Christians*. Phillipsburg, NJ: P & R Publishing. 1999.

Robinson, Haddon. *Decision Making by the Book*. Wheaton, IL: Victor Books. 1991.

Warren, Rick. *The Purpose Driven Church*. Grand Rapids, MI: Zondervan Publishing House. 1995.

Webber, Malcolm. *From Eternity to Eternity*. Goshen, IN: Pioneer Books. 1995.

Strategic Press
www.StrategicPress.org

Strategic Press is a division of Strategic Global Assistance, Inc.
www.sgai.org

513 S. Main St. Suite 2
Elkhart, IN 46516
U.S.A

+1-574-295-4357
Toll-free: 888-258-7447

www.ingramcontent.com/pod-product-compliance
Lightning Source LLC
Chambersburg PA
CBHW071814090426
42737CB00012B/2077